MW01254690

THE
PHILADELPHIA
Nativist
Riots

IRISH KENSINGTON ERUPTS

KENNETH W. MILANO

THE
History
PRESS

OUTRAGE, RIOTS, AND BLOODSHED !

BURNING OF HOUSES AND CHURCHES.

Men Shot Dead in the Streets !---City and Districts under Martial Law !

Arrival of Gov. Porter, Military from the adjacent Towns, etc. etc

FULL PARTICULAR

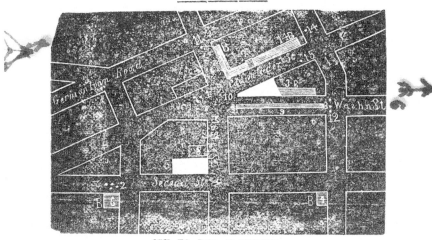

KEY TO THE ENGRAVING:

5. Lot where the first meeting was held.
9. The Market House where the meeting adjourned to.
7. Hibernia Hose House, from which the first volley of musketry was fired into the meeting.
10. Open lot across which they fired.
8. Master Street School.
11. Place where Shiffler was shot on Monday afternoon,
6. Seminary.
2. Place where Wright, Ramsey, and others were shot, on Monday night.
1. Place where Grebble, Rinedollar, and others were shot, on Tuesday afternoon.
4. St. Michael's Church.
12. The place where Col. Albright and others were shot.
13. The place where Matthew Hammett was shot.
14. The position from which the boy fired a pistol and shot one of the principal Irish rioters, while he was in the act of firing a musket from the corner marked (15.)
*. The place where Rice (an Irish Catholic) was killed, while in the act of firing, for the third time, on the Native Americans.
B. Blocks of Houses that were burned.

Contemporary broadside and only known map of Kensington Riots. *Courtesy of Daniel Dailey.*

Published by The History Press
Charleston, SC 29403
www.historypress.net

Cover: [Perry, John B.] *A Full and Complete Account of the Late Awful Riots in Philadelphia: Embellished with Ten Engraving[s]*. Philadelphia: John B. Perry, no. 198 Market Street. Henry Jordan, Third and Dock Street. New York: Nafis & Cornish, 1844.

Unless otherwise noted, all images are in the collection of the author.

First published 2013

ISBN 978-1-5402-2153-7

Library of Congress CIP data applied for.

This book is dedicated to those Irish Catholics, known and unknown, who gave their lives for their religion during Kensington's Anti-Catholic Riots of 1844. Their names may be lost to us, but their memory will never be forgotten.

Contents

ACKNOWLEDGEMENTS

This book would not have been possible without the help and support of a good number of people. As usual, my colleagues in Kensington and Fishtown history, Rich Remer and Torben Jenk, were very helpful; in particular, Torben was pressed into action to create six new maps for this publication. Daniel Dailey, whose collection of Kensingtoniana has surpassed even my own, was again generous in loaning material to one of my book projects, and I thank him. In addition, Daniel helped to sponsor the final research of this project; without his help, this project would not have been completed. I would like to thank Ned Donaghue for providing me with the quote from the Drinker diaries, and I would also like to thank Bill Askins for introducing me to the work of fellow Kensingtonian John T. McIntyre. My fellow members of the St. Anne's Historical Committee (Father Edward Brady, Cormac Brady, Lou Ferraro, Claire Gardiner, Tom Lyons, Drew Monaghan, Russ Wylie and advisors Thomas Prince and Andy Waskie) have all helped to stimulate my interest in Irish Catholic history through our work on that committee. Cormac Brady, a native-born Irishman, helped with some surname questions, which was helpful. The good folks at St. Michael's Rectory were generous to allow me to tour the cemetery and take some photographs, and Gerry Burns, in particular, helped to answer some questions about the church's history. Anita Sheahan Coraluzzi of the Genealogical Society of Pennsylvania made herself available to pick her brain on some Irish surname questions, and I thank her. The History Press has always been a wonderful company to work with, and I thank them for sticking with me, for this, my sixth book. In particular, I thank my editor Hannah Cassilly, who helped push the project along.

Note from the map creator: The buildings and courts are placed as best as described in the newspaper and trial testimony accounts, with the help of property records and city directories. The names indicate either ownership or residency, or co-owners. Some buildings have been left out for a better perception and view of the locations of the rioting.

Note for the index: The index is not a "complete" index. Rather, it lists the more important personalities of the riots, those killed and military involved, as well as many of the locations, with some subjects, etc. For those searching for genealogical purposes, it is suggested to read, or scan, the entire text.

CHAPTER I

IRELAND IN THE LATE EIGHTEENTH CENTURY

It is hard for us to imagine today the misery of what the Irish Catholics have had to endure for centuries under English rule. From the Norman invasion of the late twelfth century to the conquest by the Tudors of England that set up Protestant plantations in Ireland in the sixteenth century, Ireland has experienced what seems like constant repression and counter rebellion among its people against those who would seek to keep their foot on her throat. The settling of these Protestant plantations by the crown of England was an attempt to once and for all subdue Ireland. However, rebellions were not suppressed by these actions, as there were the Irish Confederate Wars of 1641–53 and the later Williamite War of 1689–91.

The Irish Confederate Wars started in 1641 with the Irish Catholics getting the upper hand and slaughtering thousands of Scots and English settlers in Ulster. The war took place during the confusion of the English Civil Wars. Eventually, the Irish Catholics for a short time were able to rule Ireland as a "de facto" state. However, once the English Civil War settled down, Oliver Cromwell led an invasion and re-conquest of Ireland in 1649, which was completed by 1653. By the war's end, one-third of Ireland's prewar population was dead or exiled. Cromwell imposed harsh punishments; Catholicism was banned, Irish leaders were executed or exported to the West Indies and vast amounts of the better quality remaining lands, owned by Irish Catholics, were confiscated and given to British settlers. Thus began another round of settlements of plantations in Ireland, which went as far as banning Catholics from living in towns.

During the Williamite War, Catholic King James II fought against Protestant King William to see who would claim the throne for rule over Ireland, England and Scotland. The famous Battle of the Boyne took place during the Williamite War in 1690 in Ireland. This battle, won by King William, turned the tide in the war to the Protestants' favor, thus setting up more than two centuries of Protestant rule. It was also this battle that continues to be celebrated annually by the Orangemen, to honor King William, the Prince of Orange, and a battle that later generations of Irish Protestants would sing about as they destroyed St. Michael's Church in Kensington in May 1844 during the Nativist Riots.

As we know from history, the influx of more Protestants in Ireland may have temporarily stabilized English rule, but eventually, it simply stirred the pot of troubles. When King William defeated King James II, it helped to usher in the Glorious Revolution in England, and with the ascendency of the Protestant king, things did quiet down and a relative calm came over Ireland, which lasted for most of the eighteenth century. However, even this could not last.

As the Anglo-Irish ruling class began to see Ireland as their native country, agitation started for a more favorable status with England. In particular, reform was looked at for enfranchising Irish Catholics. The American Revolution, followed by the French Revolution, inspired the Irish. In 1791, the United Irishmen were founded by mainly Presbyterian middle-class Irish. Seeing that their attempts to unify Ireland for real reform was not going to work out, they became determined to use force to overthrow the British. This activity resulted in the attempted Rebellion of 1798, which failed and was put down brutally by the English. According to historian Raymond D. Adams, within three weeks, thirty thousand people throughout Ireland, including women and children, "armed only with pitchforks and pikes, were decimated." In County Down, they were shot down and "left unburied in the streets." The leaders of the two main Ulster risings, Henry Joy McCracken and Henry Munro, were promptly executed. The "crushing defeat of the 1798 Rebellion promoted a wide-spread fear of draconian reprisals and persecution by the crown." Many of the United Irishmen fled Ireland to America, with a good number winding up in Philadelphia.

The 1790s also saw pitched battles between the Irish Catholic Defenders and the Irish Protestants' "Peep of Day Boys," thus becoming yet another decade of the long sad history of Ireland. Despite the efforts of groups like the United Irishmen, the eighteenth century ended with the founding of the

Orange Order, also known as the Orangemen, a Protestant group that was against any sort of unity with Ireland's Catholics.

It is said that in the early years of political parties in America, the Irish tended to side with the Jeffersonian Republicans, so it is not that surprising when historian Margaret H. McAleer tells us that in the late eighteenth century, Federalist Party member Peter Van Schaak thought that "early education and participation in the American Revolution had made native-born Americans more wise and virtuous than any other people on earth and therefore better qualified to administer and support a Republican Government than immigrants born under other regimes." This statement was in response to recently arrived Irishman Daniel Clark, who in 1799 listed an advertisement in a Philadelphia paper for a meeting of the American Society of United Irishmen. The group was founded a couple years earlier after many members of Ireland's United Irishmen fled to America. Ireland's United Irishmen were initially interested in parliamentary reform in Ireland and tried to unite both Irish Catholics and Protestants in this cause. However, influenced by the American and French Revolutions, they attempted their own rebellion in 1798, which failed.

Forty-five years later, the Native American Party would put forth a similar argument that the recent Irish immigrants should have to have spent twenty-one years in America before they would be allowed to vote or take part in politics. At the time, one had to be twenty-one years old to vote, and the nativists thought it would take these new immigrants that long (twenty-one years) to understand what it meant to be an American. McAleer goes on to state that over "ten thousand Irish immigrants landed in ports in the Delaware (River) region during the final decade of the eighteenth century" and that "many of these immigrants had participated in, or at least witnessed radical political events in Ireland." Some of these immigrants had even been "members of largely lower-class agrarian and urban groups, like the Defenders, which married grievances over high rents, tithes, and taxes, with half-digested French principles and an anti-ascendancy political ideology." Others joined the United Irishmen.

Dennis Clark, a historian on the Irish in Philadelphia, makes a point that "the impact of the Irish on the politics of the city during the early nineteenth century extended beyond alarms and agitation. They were adding a new dimension to politics, a dimension that was to help in the evolution of the party system." By the beginning of the nineteenth century, Clark estimates that there were five thousand Irish born in the city, and "many of these were veterans of the Irish Volunteers, a group that had helped to lead the failed uprising in Ireland in 1798." When this uprising was rebuffed, many of these Irish had to flee Ireland, resulting in many immigrating to Philadelphia.

The violence against the Irish Catholics perpetrated by the nativists during the Kensington Riots of 1844 was very similar to those actions taken by Ireland's County Armagh's "Peep of Day Boys" (founded circa 1784) who secured a victory over the Defenders (Irish Catholics who resisted Protestant aggression) in 1795 at the Battle of the Diamond. The Peep of Day Boys attacked Irish Catholic homes at the "peep of day," broke open the doors of their homes, smashed anything and everything of value, tossed it out into the street and, in many cases, burnt the houses. Also, much like the nativists using the pretext of searching for arms to invade Irish Catholic houses in Kensington, the Peep of Day Boys took these same actions against the Catholics in Ireland. The Peep of Day Boys were made up of Anglicans and Presbyterians, similar to their nativist counterparts in Kensington.

Estimates put upward of thirty Defenders killed at the Battle of the Diamond. This victory led to the founding of the Orange Order ("the Orangemen"), and over the course of the 1790s, the group was able to murder, frighten and drive out up to seven thousand Irish Catholics from central Ulster. Groups like the Peep of Day Boys and the Orange Order helped to turn Ireland into various sects fighting each other, which offset the unity ideas of the United Irishmen. These groups also acted in conjunction with the British in suppressing the United Irishmen's Rebellion of 1798.

It was with this backdrop that many of the Irish immigrated to Philadelphia in the last decade of the eighteenth century and the first two decades of the nineteenth century, founding the Irish Catholic community of West Kensington. It is no surprise that many of the early Irish of this community had Ulster surnames.

CHAPTER 2

THE FOUNDING OF THE IRISH CATHOLIC COMMUNITY OF WEST KENSINGTON

The red carpet was not exactly waiting for the Irish Catholics when they immigrated to Philadelphia. Prejudices already existed against the Irish Catholics, even in a place like William Penn's "Holy Experiment." In her diary, Elizabeth Drinker, of an old prominent Quaker family, makes the following observation about St. Patrick's Day in Philadelphia in 1798, the year of the failed United Irishmen rebellion: "The old foolish custom of carriing [sic] Paddys about is not yet done with, the boys are noisey at it this evening..."

In her footnote to the text of Drinker's diary, Elaine Forman Crane, the editor of the published diaries of Drinker, comments that historians Scharf and Wescott quoted the following in their monumental work on the history of Philadelphia:

> *Effigies* [were] *constructed by Irish Protestants, and sometimes by American-born Philadelphians, to the consternation and anger of the city's Irish Catholic residents. Stuffed with old clothes and straw, the paddies had strings of potatoes hung around their necks, pipes stuck in their mouths, and bottles placed in one hand and glasses in the other. They were carried to Irish areas before daybreak on St. Patrick's Day and hung by their necks from trees or awning posts.*

This is the sort of behavior the Irish Catholics could expect as they left their mother country and came to America to start a "new" life. It's hard to imagine it today, but much like African Americans were discriminated against in American history, so too were the Irish Catholics. Philadelphia's illustrious history proved this in a big way when the Anti-Irish Catholic Riots of May 1844 broke out, destroying the physical Kensington Irish Catholic neighborhood but not its faith or heart. The Irish, like the Italians, Eastern European Poles and Jews in the later nineteenth century, had to fight for respect in American society, and while the Irish and African Americans often battled each other in nineteenth-century Philadelphia, it was generally due to the fact that they lived among each other and competed for the same housing and jobs. Wherever there was an Irish Catholic neighborhood, it was usually adjacent to an African American community.

In Philadelphia, the Irish Catholics tended to live among themselves for the first several generations before being absorbed into the melting pot. Unlike Germans, or other Anglos from Northern Europe, the Irish Catholics in Philadelphia lived in just several neighborhoods in the nineteenth century. A study done by Miriam Eisenhardt, Jeffrey Sultanik and Alan Berman titled *The Five Irish Clusters in 1880 Philadelphia* takes a look at these nineteenth-century neighborhoods. The three University of Pennsylvania students, under the guidance of Alan Burstein (resident demographer of the Philadelphia Social History Project), showed that Irish immigrants clustered in five distinct neighborhoods of Philadelphia. This study was on the Irish of 1880, more than thirty years after the Nativist Riots, but the five Irish neighborhoods in 1880 were Irish in earlier years as well.

Southwest of Center City (or what is sometimes called Schuylkill or Gray's Ferry) was the largest of the Irish neighborhoods. Remnants of this neighborhood still exist in Tannytown (Twenty-sixth and South Streets area) and Gray's Ferry. Today's Fitler Square would have been included in this area. This Irish neighborhood was bordered on the south by one of the largest African American neighborhoods of Philadelphia.

The area just northwest of Center City, north of Vine Street and west of Broad Street to the Schuylkill River, was another Irish neighborhood. It was called Spring Garden, later Fairmount, and now it is called the "Art Museum Area." In this area, African Americans were again bordering the Irish neighborhood, along Ridge Avenue to the east, further evidence that African Americans and Irish Catholics were huddled together in Philadelphia.

The neighborhood of Southwark (southeast of Center City), called "Queen's Village" today, was another Irish area. The remnants of this area can be seen among the Irish of the "Two Street" neighborhood, or Second Street south of Washington Avenue. In 1880, this Irish neighborhood would have encompassed everything south of Spruce Street from Tenth Street to the Delaware River. This was the time before Jewish and Italian immigration filled the northern and western edges of this community. African Americans were also strong in this area, particularly along Lombard, South and Bainbridge Streets.

Since the city of Philadelphia originally only went from Vine Street as the northern border to South Street as the southern border, it would have been normal for the patricians of the city to push the African Americans and Irish Catholics from the city proper. Thus, the above three Irish and African American communities sat on the outskirts of the (pre-1854) city proper and remained that way for most of the nineteenth century.

The other two Irish Catholic neighborhoods were also outside of the city proper. Frankford was the fourth Irish cluster and was a very Irish neighborhood, with almost 75 percent of the people being Irish in 1880, while Kensington was the fifth Irish cluster—in particular, Kensington west of Frankford Avenue and north of Girard, centered around St. Michael's Church at Second and Jefferson Streets. The Fishtown area of Kensington would not have its own Irish Catholic church until Holy Name opened in 1905. By then, many of the Protestant churches, their congregations dwindling, began moving out of the area, and eventually, Fishtown came to be very much an Irish Catholic community. Of these five Irish clusters, Kensington was the area that had the most skilled of the Irish immigrants, many of them being weavers, while their counterparts in the other Irish districts were laborers, carters or coal heavers.

While Frankford's Irish had a small African American community living among them (a free black pre–Civil War community east of Frankford Avenue), Kensington, on the other hand, never appears to have had an African American community of any size in the nineteenth century, unless you count the several families centered around Frankford and Norris Streets, where porters for the railroad at the Kensington Depot (Front & Berks) lived, or the several families that once lived along Howard Street north of Girard Avenue.

Turner Camac and the Breakup of the Masters Estate

The Irish Catholic neighborhood that surrounded the Nanny Goat Market in West Kensington has no specific date for its founding. Rather, the neighborhood developed over the course of the twenty-year period from 1810 to 1830. A good bit of this neighborhood was the old Masters family estate "Green Spring," later called the "Camac Estate." The entire estate was situated roughly between today's Girard Avenue and Montgomery Street, and Point Pleasant (Frankford and the Delaware River) to just past Broad Street. According to Kensington historian Rich Remer, "Turner Camac arrived at Point Pleasant (Kensington) from England, determined to manage profitably the surrounding Masters Estate owned by his wife, Sarah Masters, and her sister Mary, the wife of Richard Penn, grandson of the founder and one time proprietor of Pennsylvania, William Penn." Camac quickly overcame years of "local mismanagement and within a few years had restored profitability." It was during this twenty-year period that the Irish Catholic neighborhood of West Kensington came to be founded.

According to Remer, Sarah was married to Turner Camac (1751–1830) in 1795. At that time, she was living in England. She, her sister Mary and Richard Penn left Philadelphia before the British occupation of the city during the Revolution. They left their lands in the hands of overseers. While living in England, Sarah was introduced to Camac, and they married. Camac left England about 1804 and immigrated to America. His wife's estate was a very valuable estate but poorly mismanaged. The estate at that time bordered the northern edge of the growing metropolis of Philadelphia and included a good portion of today's neighborhoods of Northern Liberties, West Kensington and North Philadelphia. Sarah had received her share of her father's estate a number of years after her father died, but by the 1790s, the sheriff was already starting to seize her property in lieu of taxes. Camac was able to put the estate in order. He sold properties for a profit, sold off ones that were not useful, rented out others, made sure rents were paid on time and collected the back rents. He even built some businesses of his own. In a short time, the estate was considered very valuable.

The Masters sisters were the daughters of William Masters, a one-time mayor of Philadelphia, who himself inherited the estate from his father, Thomas Masters. Thomas Masters started to put together his estate as early as 1714 when he purchased the "Governor's Mill," which was located roughly at today's Third Street and Girard Avenue. The estate eventually grew to upward of six hundred acres. Sarah and Mary inherited their shares of the estate in 1775. Sarah Masters wound up with the parcels that would eventually become St. Michael's Church, Hugh and Patrick Clark's homes and the Cadwalader Street area of the riots. Her sister Mary came to own the property that became the Master Street School and the nunnery of St. Michael's.

According to an online one-name study of the surname Camac, we find out that Turner Camac came from a rather illustrious family:

> *In Ireland, several members of the Camac family were from Lurgan, County Louth, and went into service with the Honorable East India Company (HEICS) and made a considerable fortune in the 18th century. One of these gentlemen, Jacob Camac (1745–1784) commanded the 24th (Ramgarh) Infantry that subdued the districts of Ramgarh, Palamau and Chota Nagpur, over which the HEICS gave him political control. He brutally suppressed a Sepoy rebellion and had an illegitimate daughter Eliza Marian Camac (1775–1804) by the Princess Marionissa of Mysore, niece of Hyder Ali and a cousin of Tippo Sahib. His father John Camac and brother Turner Camac (1751–1830) owned copper mines in County Wicklow, Ireland and in 1792 minted the "Camac" Pennies, halfpennies and farthings. Turner Camac was also a founder and director of the Grand Canal Company in 1791, causing him to be commemorated by the still extant "Camac Bridge" in Dublin. Turner Camac immigrated to Philadelphia in 1804 and was a volunteer sergeant in the 1812 War.*

Turner Camac and his wife lived stylishly at a mansion house at what today would be the northeast corner of Eleventh and Montgomery Streets (they also had a townhouse in the city at 152 South Third Street). According to a description of the country house that was written up for a painting executed by David J. Kennedy in 1838, "it was a beautiful spot surrounded by old forest trees with a sloping lawn to the north, the entrance to it was by Camac (Cecil B. Moore) Lane from Broad Street north to Monument Cemetery, the lane was bordered by rows of fir trees and from Girard Avenue north and as far as east as Fifth Street it was open country, fields of grain, cattle pasture, etc." The house was sketched by Kennedy in 1838, and the home was demolished in 1870. Turner Camac died about 1830, having given quite a boost in helping to found West Kensington's Irish Catholic neighborhood. It was the "Camac Woods" on his property that many Irish Catholics fled to when their homes were destroyed and fired by the nativist mobs in May 1844.

DEVELOPMENT OF THE NANNY GOAT MARKET NEIGHBORHOOD

When breaking up the Masters Estate, Camac appears to have laid out Master Street as one of the earliest streets in the West Kensington neighborhood. Master Street was formerly called Timber Lane (1811 Philadelphia City Directory) and may have already been in use when Camac arrived in Philadelphia, though not officially laid out. We can assume the name Master Street was used to honor the family.

When alderman and Irish Catholic leader Hugh Clark first bought his house in West Kensington at the southwest corner of Fourth and Master Streets on May 2, 1828, he and his brother Patrick purchased the lot and house from Turner Camac. Camac had been renting the property to Martin Foulke, a farmer of the Northern Liberties, since about 1812. This property had been one of the properties seized by the sheriff from Sarah Masters's estate and rescued by Turner Camac. This dwelling house of the Clark brothers would later be sacked by the nativists during the riots.

Could it have been that Turner Camac, an Irishman himself, helped to promote this area to his fellow Irishmen, thus leading to its becoming an Irish Catholic neighborhood? Camac was a member of the Church of England but sympathized with Irish Catholics. Upon news of the passage of the Emancipation Act (for Catholics) by the English Parliament in 1829, a great celebration took place at the statehouse (Independence Hall) in Philadelphia, where Camac, along with other Irish Catholic leaders like Matthew Carey, presided over the celebration. He had previously been chairman of a group that conducted a "meeting of friends of civil and religious freedom in Ireland." He was considered very liberal-minded.

In an earlier newspaper article in the *National Gazette* of November 6, 1828, there is mention of Philadelphians donating monies to the "New Catholic Association of Ireland," an organization founded to help emancipate all of the Irish. Turner Camac was a large supporter of this cause and wrote a letter to Irish political leader Daniel O'Connell, which he included along with the money raised (over £182). O'Connell responded in kind with the following words about Camac:

> *This gentleman in the year '92, was one of the grand jury for the county Louth, and the only one who did not agree to the petition then drawn up against the Byrnes, the Keoghs, and the Catholics of the day (against enfranchisement of Catholics). Probably he is the sole survivor of that*

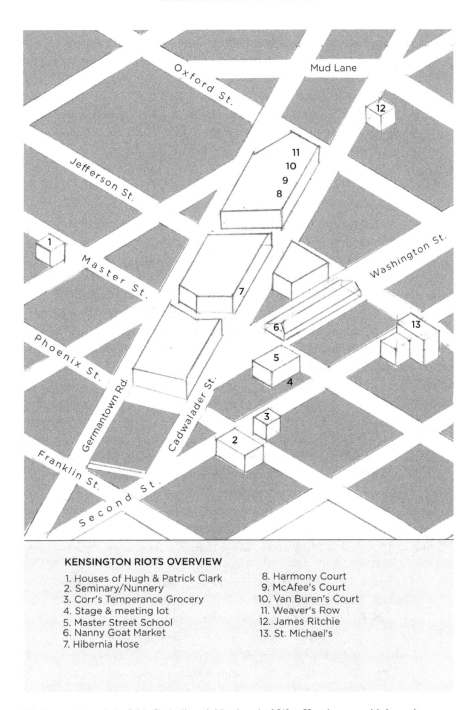

KENSINGTON RIOTS OVERVIEW

1. Houses of Hugh & Patrick Clark
2. Seminary/Nunnery
3. Corr's Temperance Grocery
4. Stage & meeting lot
5. Master Street School
6. Nanny Goat Market
7. Hibernia Hose

8. Harmony Court
9. McAfee's Court
10. Van Buren's Court
11. Weaver's Row
12. James Ritchie
13. St. Michael's

Bird's-eye view of the Irish Catholic neighborhood of West Kensington, with legend showing significant buildings, streets and courtyards. *Courtesy Torben Jenk.*

grand jury, unless happily indeed, Lord Oriel was one amongst them, who has now lived to see the bigotry of his family exposed, themselves despised and driven from their native country, while all Ireland now hails the patriotic name of Turner Camac, which now reaches them over the waves of the Atlantic. In patriotic task, Mr. Camac has been joined by many gentlemen, who have quitted the green fields of Erin, and melancholy and sad must their hearts have been, when they left this lovely land.

Camac was from Greenmount Lodge, in County Louth, Ireland. Besides his interests in copper mines and canals, Camac was high sheriff for a time of County Louth. The famous Battle of the Boyne took place in Louth. However, Camac was seen as a friend of Catholics, which put him in a difficult position in the 1790s when the United Irishmen rebellion began.

Camac's mining operations in Ireland consisted of his and his brother's capital being pumped into a partnership with the Hibernian Mining Company of John Howard Kyan, which was in competition with a British-owned mining company in the valley of the Avoca River in County Wicklow. The companies competed against each other in issuing copper coins or half-penny tokens. While the Camac brothers' capital helped keep the mine afloat, it was not successful. By 1797, the mine was terminated, with Kyan dying penniless, his son having to go to work in a factory. It is stated that £60,000 was expended on the mine (1787–97). The Camac brothers appear to have taken a terrible loss, and Turner Camac just may have been looking for an alternative plan for his future when he married Mary Masters in 1795.

Not only was Camac possibly looking for a brighter economic opportunity, but he also may have wanted to leave a dangerous political situation. According to a study of the Arco River–area mining operations, the rivalry between Camac's Hibernian Mining Company and the English Associated Mining Company was expressed in more than just their coinage:

The rivalry between the Hibernian Mining Company and the English Associated Irish Mining Company (AIMC) as expressed in their coinage may have had deeper social and political dimensions. Kyan and Camac had apparently given employment in 1792 to a number of Defenders (Irish Catholics) who had been driven out of County Louth. As national and local tensions rose in 1796 the Hibernian Mining Company set up two corps of yeomanry—the Castlemacadam Calvary (commanded by Turner Camac) and the Castlemacadam Calvary (commanded by his brother James) the local gentry was highly suspicious about these, one comment being that they were potentially "the most dangerous body of men to the peace of the country." There were grounds for such apprehensions: the Camacs were suspected of republican sympathies and their partner Kyan was a close kinsman of Esmond Kyan of Wexford, a local leader of the United Irishmen. That a significant number of this yeomanry was actively involved in the United Irishmen was clearly established by early 1798, it was, for instance, reported that the Hibernian Mining Companies workers had selected one James McQuillan, alias James Collins, to tour the area acting as an agent provocateur, stirring up local Orangemen in order to find out what their real plans were. He was discovered and in March 1798 both the Camac's infantry and Calvary Corp's comprising Ballymurtagh miners were formally disbanded.

Politically and economically, Turner Camac may very well have decided that his time in Ireland was up and immigration to Philadelphia was the best thing for him and his family. County Louth bordered Ulster Province, and many Irish Catholics sought safety in the bordering counties of Ulster after the United Irishmen's failed rebellion in 1798. Many of their leaders were from County Louth, and many of the early residents of West Kensington had Ulster surnames, so it may not have been a coincidence that West Kensington developed as it did—as an Irish Catholic neighborhood on land connected to a friend of Irish Catholics, Turner Camac. He very well may have looked to help his fellow countrymen who left Ireland as he did by settling them in Philadelphia and, in turn, help himself with the profits of the development of his wife's estate.

Besides Master Street, there was not an east–west street laid out in West Kensington in the early nineteenth century. Two landed estates encompassing over 1,200 acres (the Masters Estate on the southern side of West Kensington and the Norris' Fairhill Estate on the northern side) stalled development until the breakup of these estates began with the Masters Estate in the 1810s and the Fairhill Estate in the 1840s.

The District of Kensington itself was not established until March 6, 1820, and until that time, it had come under the jurisdiction of the Northern Liberties Township, which tended to be controlled politically by men from the Northern Liberties District. On April 15, 1834, Kensington was first sectioned off into five different wards. The West Kensington neighborhood around the Nanny Goat Market at Washington (American) and Master Streets became known as Kensington's Third Ward. The Third Ward encompassed the area bounded by Front Street on the east, Sixth Street on the west, Franklin (Girard Avenue) Street on the south and Montgomery Street on the north. The Nanny Goat Market and St. Michael's Church sat roughly in the center of this ward. The Third Ward quickly became an Irish Catholic neighborhood centered on these two institutions. The boundaries of the Third Ward stayed intact from 1834 until 1846, when the ward was split into two (Third and Sixth Wards, with Second Street as the dividing line) as more and more Irish Catholics poured into the neighborhood even after the riots of '44.

The first notable street in the Nanny Goat Market neighborhood would have been Germantown Road (later Avenue), which was earlier laid out and developed. In the first decade of the nineteenth century, most of Kensington's north–south numbered streets only went as far north as Germantown Road. Germantown Road, Old York Road (Fifth Street) and Frankford Road were the streets to take you north of the city. There were no houses to speak of west of Fifth Street in the early nineteenth century, and north of Montgomery Street was mostly farm lands and the Norris family estate and gardens of Fairhill.

After Master Street was put through the area, residents began to petition the courts for laying out additional streets. Turner Camac, while suffering monetary damages when streets were ordered open (he was paid for his land, but sometimes not at the price he desired), did eventually benefit because he could then offer smaller home lots on newly opened streets. One of the first of the east–west streets to be petitioned to open was Phoenix (Thompson) Street. In 1830, it was proposed to open the street from Frankford Avenue to Old York Road (Fifth Street). From Frankford to Germantown, the street was to be called Phoenix; from Germantown to Old York Road, it was to be called Thompson. Hugh Clark—alderman, manufacturer and police magistrate of Kensington's Third Ward Irish—was one person who wanted the road opened. Opposing Clark and the others were several people led by Jacob Dutton, who stated that the road would damage greatly his ropewalk (Dutton Street) as well as two other ropewalks in the path of the proposed road. Henry Crilly, who owned property along the proposed new road, was awarded $450 in damages. Crilly and Clark were two of the founders of St. Michael's Church and leaders of the Irish Catholics of Kensington. Crilly had owned property around Germantown and Phoenix since at least 1827.

Cadwalader Street very well may have been in use early on as the back alley for the homes and business on the east side of Germantown Avenue, but in 1830, a formal petition was entered in court asking for the opening of the street, and by 1831, it was opened. While there were no names of

Photographs are lacking for Kensington's courtyards and back alleys, but this photo from New York City gives one an idea of their appearance and "friendliness."

the founders of St. Michael's listed on the petition to open the street, it was peppered with Irish names like Bernard Sherry, John and Patrick Quinn, James Donahoe and others. Sherry would later suffer in the riots to the tune of $3,000 in damages, having four houses on Cadwalader Street destroyed and burned, as well as being arrested in the rioting. He was said to be a master weaver and one of the leaders of the Irish Catholics during the riots. He was arrested for arming his workmen to fight the nativists. Cadwalader Street between Master and Oxford was the main combat area of the riots. On this street, between Jefferson and Oxford, were four courtyards where many of the rioters lived and operated.

Jefferson Street, the street that served as the northern border for the Nanny Goat Market, was petitioned to be opened from Front Street to Sixth Street in 1831. Soon after, a petition for the opening of Washington Street was approved on July 6, 1832. Washington Street is today's American Street. It was also the street where the Nanny Goat Market was erected in 1835. Of the

Vault of Michael Keenan (1797–1862), St. Michael's Cemetery. A boss weaver and one of the founders of St. Michael's Church, his property was fired during the riots.

seventeen men whose names were on the petition to open Washington Street, four of them were founders of St. Michael's Church: William Browning, Hugh Clark, Henry Crilly and Michael Keenan. Both Clark and Keenan would suffer property losses in the riots. Along with Clark and his co-founders, a number of the others who signed the petition for Washington Street appear to have Irish-sounding surnames. Charles Elliott, a dry goods merchant, was one of the petitioners. He owned three houses on Harmony Court (east from Cadwalader above Jefferson Street) that were fired and destroyed by the nativists during the Kensington Riots, as Harmony Court was headquarters for the Irish rioters on May 7. Patrick Murray, another petitioner, would later have his store at Jefferson and Germantown sacked and set on fire during the riots, a loss of $4,000. He had aided the Irish Catholics by supplying them with ammunition. Murray owned the lot of land that sat on Jefferson Street from Germantown Road through to Cadwalader Street.

Washington Street was to be opened from Master Street north to Montgomery Street (above Montgomery was mainly farm land). The original plan was to have Washington Street come as far south as today's Girard Avenue, hitting Girard Avenue at a right angle, like most of William Penn's orderly city. However, there were many who complained about the street coming this far south, and apparently they won out. Oddly enough, or perhaps not, many petitioning to have Washington Street opened all the way were Irish immigrants who owned land above Girard Avenue. The ones in opposition had surnames that appeared to indicate they were not Irish Catholics, perhaps American born, who owned land south of Master Street, perhaps an early sign of agitation in the neighborhood between the newly arrived Irish and their American-born counterparts.

Before the riots of 1844, the triangular lot that sat between the Nanny Goat Market and Cadwalader Street (today's Crane Building) was for the most part not developed, and neither was the lot on the east side of the market house. Within ten years of the riot, the triangular property was built up, a large piece of it owned by Bernard Sherry (a sufferer in the riots) and Michael Magill (probably Michael McGill, a founder of St. Michael's).

FOUNDING OF ST. MICHAEL'S CHURCH

At the founding of St. Michael's Church in 1831, there was hardly a Roman Catholic east of Frankford Avenue and north of Shackamaxon. East Kensington (today's Fishtown) was staunchly Protestant and very loud about it. Until St. Michael's Church was founded in 1831, there was no Catholic church in Kensington. Most Catholics of the area were forced to travel some distance to attend mass, be baptized or get married. The registers of St. Augustine Church, on Fourth Street below Vine, show the names of a number of residents of Kensington who made that church their place of worship.

In April 1831, eight men gathered at the home of John Waters on Front Street above Callowhill. This meeting was the first meeting of what would become the trustees of St. Michael's Church. Two of the men at this meeting were Bishop Coadjutor Francis Patrick Kenrick and Reverend John Hughes, the future archbishop of New York City, a man whose tongue and pen were said to be feared by the nativists. He is credited with putting a stop to the threat of nativism in New York City. He would become quite prominent, a friend of presidents, ambassador extraordinaire to the court of Napoleon III and an advisor to the secretary of state during the Civil War.

Earliest known illustration of St. Michael's Church and parish buildings, all destroyed during the riots, taken from *Old St. Michael's: The Story, 1834–1944* (Philadelphia: Jefferies & Manz, 1934).

Reverend Hughes's charge at the time of this meeting in 1831 was St. John's Catholic Church on Thirteenth Street below Market. He acted as a trustee for St. Michael's until a pastor was appointed. The other six men at the meeting were laymen and leaders of the Irish Catholics of Kensington and the Northern Liberties: John Waters, Henry Crilly, Adam Miller, Patrick McBride, Hugh Clark and William Browning.

By the 1830s, the area east of the Germantown Road was fairly developed and Second Street became a prime route into the city. Thus it was here that the founders and original trustees of St. Michael's Church decided to locate their church in 1831 by purchasing a lot from the Camac family (William M. Camac, esq., son of Turner Camac) at Jefferson and Second Streets for $3,333. This lot extended from Second Street to Hancock Street and from Jefferson south 143 feet toward Phoenix Street. The trustees organized a building committee made up of other Irish Catholic leaders of Kensington and the Northern Liberties: Bernard Maguire, Michael McGill, Michael Keenan, Patrick Murphy, Richard McAvoy and Edward McQuade. Further ground would later be bought from the Camac family in order to expand the cemetery, and a large rectory was built in 1839, costing over $4,000. In his diary, Reverend Francis Patrick Kenrick states that on June 12, 1831, he "blessed solemnly, according to the rite of the Pontifical, the cemetery of St. Michael's in Kensington. About two thousand people, or more, were present." The cemetery would be vandalized and the rectory totally destroyed by fire during the riots.

The cornerstone of the church was laid by the Reverend Francis Patrick Kendrick on April 8, 1833, assisted by nine other priests, including the Reverend Terence J. Donaghoe, who was appointed the new pastor of the church. Donaghoe was a native of Aughnacloy, County Tyrone, which was not far from the future archbishop John Hughes's hometown of Annaloghan. In fact, the two attended school together in Ireland. Before his appointment to the newly built St. Michael's, Donaghoe had previously been a pastor at Philadelphia's St. Joseph's for three years. After his new appointment, he soon rented a house on Fourth Street above Franklin (Girard). While living here, the trustees would sometimes meet at his home, and he would say mass during the week. On Sundays, services would be offered at Patrick McBride's house. Once the building of the church was advanced enough, Father Donaghoe moved into the sacristy in the spring of 1834. The church was officially dedicated on September 28, 1834, by Bishop Kendrick. It is said that the church was built in the Gothic style, without buttresses, but others say it was rather plain. The interior was graced with a painting of St. Michael the Archangel by Guido Reni. This painting had formerly been in the collection of Joseph Cardinal Fesch, archbishop of Lyons and half brother to Napoleon's mother. The painting was destroyed when the church burned during the riots. Valued at $3,000, the church received $1,000 in compensation from the County. For the destruction of the church, the County paid St. Michael's $27,000. This dollar value was less than the cost of the bare buildings that were destroyed.

A chance accidental meeting led to the erection of St. Michael's Convent, the "nunnery," as it was called in the press during the riots. Mrs. Margaret McDonough (mother of Lieutenant McDonough, a hero of the War of 1812, and grandmother of John O'Brien, brevet major and a hero at Buena Vista) was a friend of Father Donaghoe. In 1833, it was to Mrs. McDonough's house that five ladies from Ireland ventured (Frances Clark, Margaret Mann, Rose O'Toole, Elizabeth Kelly and Catharine

Byrne). The women had been teaching at a seminary in Dublin and were encouraged by a priest from Philadelphia to come to the city for the many opportunities it afforded. Unfortunately, Miss Kelly accidentally dropped her pocketbook with the entire savings of the five women into the ocean on the trip over. Arriving penniless and not knowing what to do, they made their way to Mrs. McDonough's home, near St. Joseph's Church. In a few days they met Father Donaghoe, which in turn led him to suggest they found a religious order. They excitedly accepted and soon were placed in a rental home within St. Michael's parish and started a school at 520 North Second Street. The school was quickly a success, and lay teachers were needed to help. Father Donaghoe needed to add further classrooms, so he rented two brownstone houses farther north, on Second Street, opposite Laurel, and nearer to St. Michael's.

Within a short time, a lot of ground was acquired in July 1837 at the southeast corner of Phoenix and Second Streets, where a convent was built at a cost of slightly over $6,000 and the Order of the Sisters of Charity of the Blessed Virgin Mary was born. The Sisters had no trouble raising the money to build the convent, as well-to-do Catholics from around the city contributed. The Sisters took charge of the new convent on St. Michael's Day, September 29, 1838. They lived in the commodious convent, kept a parochial school and also offered an academy for boarding. Their work continued here until 1843, when it was decided that the order of nuns would move to Iowa. There was only one Sister and two young women in the convent when it was torched and destroyed by the nativists during the riots of May 1844. The Sisters received $6468.98 from the County for damages.

The original boundaries for St. Michael's Church was Kensington, Northern Liberties and the eastern portion of Penn Township east of Broad Street; however, the northeast was not defined, and thus people from Port Richmond, Bridesburg, Harrowgate and Frankford came to St. Michael's in the early years. The southern border was Vine Street; the western border was Broad Street, the eastern border the Delaware River. Boundaries contracted after the founding of St. Joachim's (Frankford), St. Anne's (Port Richmond) and Assumption (District of Spring Garden), all in 1845, and St. Malachy's in 1850 (Penn District).

The Founders of St. Michael's

The original trustees of St. Michael's were all laymen: John Waters (1782–1862), Henry Crilly (1793–1867), Adam Miller, Patrick McBride (1807–1868), Hugh Clark (1796–1862) and William Browning, as were the six men picked for the building committee to erect the church: Bernard Maguire (1786–1870), Michael McGill (1780–1862), Michael Keenan (1797–1862), Patrick Murphy, Richard McAvoy (1782–1860) and Edward McQuade.

These men were a virtual who's who of Irish Catholic leaders in the West Kensington and Northern Liberties communities. Henry Crilly, Michael McGill, Patrick McBride and Adam Miller were all members of the Society for the Defense of the Faith, also called the Vindicators of the Catholic Religion from Calumny and Abuse. Crilly, Keenan, McGill and Maguire were four of the forty-nine prominent Catholics to sign the petition to enforce the Resolutions of 1834 that were to leave Bible reading up to the conscience of teachers and pupils. Six of the men (Crilly, Clark, Keenan, McBride, Maguire and Waters) were members of the Friendly Sons of St. Patrick. Clark, Browning, Keenan and Waters were all manufacturers, employing a good number of the recently arrived Irish Catholic immigrant weavers. Crilly, McAvoy and McGill were grocers. Maguire was a tavern and hotel keeper. Clark was an alderman, police magistrate, a school board director, a director of the Manufacturers' and Mechanics' Bank (as was Joseph P. Norris, owner of the Fairhill Estate) and commissioner of the District of Kensington. Keenan was also a commissioner of Kensington and served on the board of the Beneficial Savings Fund, as well as being first lieutenant in the old Hibernia Greens. Crilly was one of the directors of the Kensington National Bank, director of the County Insurance Company and a manager of the Beneficial Saving Fund. At his death, Bernard Maguire donated his entire estate, about $40,000, to Catholic institutions. Almost all of the men were buried at St. Michael's Cemetery.

The New Catholic Association of Ireland was founded in Philadelphia about 1828. This group's mission statement was to promote Irish agriculture, extend commerce with Ireland, diffuse a liberal and enlightened system of education throughout Ireland, encourage the consumption of Irish manufactures, encourage as much as possible a free and enlightened press, preserve purity of elections in Ireland and establish the means of erecting churches in Ireland. Besides luminaries that one might expect to be a member, like Matthew Carey, Kensington was represented by eight of the twelve founders of St. Michael's Church: John Waters, Henry Crilly, Hugh

Celtic crosses on the tombstones in St. Michael's Cemetery. The cemetery and its burial register survived the riots, and a number of the Irish Catholic rioters rest here.

Clark, Patrick McBride, Michael Keenan, Patrick Murphy, Michael McGill and Bernard McGuire. Hugh Clark's brother Patrick and Michael Keenan's brother Edward were also members of this group.

FOUNDING OF THE NANNY GOAT MARKET

The Nanny Goat Market was said to be the heart of the Irish Catholic community of Kensington. Ever since it was established in 1835, the market place became a place where the Irish would shop, gather to meet friends and talk. A check of the 1837 Philadelphia City Directory shows that there were 142 entries in the directory for the immediate neighborhood of the Nanny Goat Market (east of Second Street to Germantown Road, Phoenix Street north to Jefferson Street), of which 83 were Irish-sounding surnames, 7 possible Irish surnames and 52 were non-Irish surnames, making the neighborhood 63 percent Irish. Almost 10 percent of these Irish had Ulster Northern Ireland surnames. Undoubtedly, the percentage might rise higher if Second Street was taken into consideration as well.

A District of Kensington ordinance of June 4, 1835, allowed for the erection of the Washington Market (its official name, though it was quickly nicknamed the "Nanny Goat Market"). The market was to be on Washington Street (later American Street) from Master Street north to Jefferson Street. The market shed was 250 feet and was built in a pavilion fashion, with a wooden roof and brick pillars to hold it. At the northern end, there were cubicles for the vendors, and at the southern end, it was more open, suitable for meetings. One source states it was on the eastern side of Washington Street.

The ordinance for the erection of the market came after the District of Kensington was petitioned by a "large number of property holders, owners, and other inhabitants" of the district. Because of the improvements being made in that area of the district, the commissioners of Kensington felt it was warranted to take immediate action on the project. The treasurer of the district was given the authority to borrow money up to $5,000, to be paid out in installments as required. The rental income from the market would be used to pay for the loan up to ten years. When the market burned down during the riots of May 1844, the District of Kensington would seem to have still been using the rental income to pay off the loan.

The market house was governed by the District of Kensington's Committee on Markets. This market was to be governed under the same rules as the earlier Beach and Maiden Streets Market (established 1820). On market days (every day but Sunday), the committee allowed the country people who were bringing the produce of their farms to market in wagons, carts, sleighs, sleds or other carriages to park on Second Street between Master Street and the southern boundary of the district (the north bank of the Cohocksink Creek). The market hours were from three hours before daylight until 3:00 p.m. (later until 4:00 p.m.). There were a number of laws governing the market house and its vendors, and a clerk was hired to enforce these laws. A police officer generally acted as the clerk, and he was entitled to his pay as an officer and as a clerk, issuing fines for any infractions. At a meeting of the District of Kensington Commissioners in 1843, Colonel Rambo was continued as the clerk of the market house.

An advertisement in the December 18, 1835 *Philadelphia Inquirer* stated that a meeting of the stockholders of the Washington Market had taken place on December 5. Charles Elliot, Esq., chairman; John A. Elkinton, secretary; and J. Pickering made up a committee that was to confer with the district commissioners about the market house. The market house meetings were held at the Bucks County Hotel at Second and Green Streets. Elkinton was a medical doctor, an alderman for Lower Delaware Ward (in the city) and a one-time port physician and a member of the board of health. While involved with the Washington Market, he does not appear to have lived in the neighborhood; rather, he lived in the city. He died in 1853 and was buried at Monument Cemetery, where he was on the board of trustees. It was not a Catholic cemetery. Charles Elliot owned three of the houses on Harmony Court that were destroyed during the riots.

Philadelphia writer George Lippard traveled the streets of West Kensington in the middle of the nineteenth century. From a novel Lippard wrote titled *The Nazarene*, we get a glimpse of what the Nanny Goat Market neighborhood might have looked and sounded like at the time of the Nativist Riots:

> *A few paces from the school-house to the east, lies Second Street. Northward on this street, not more than a hundred yards from the school-house, arises the walls of St. Michael's Church, and southward at the same distance, you may behold the Catholic Nunnery. These locations are worthy of your serious recollection, for let me tell you, in a few days this quarter of Kensington, will become the scene of strange and terrible events.*
>
> *At the corner of Master and Cadwalader, a lamp glares faintly through the mist. Leaving its dim light, we will plunge into the darkness of the alley. Here we behold a house of time-worn brick, there a toppling frame; on every side the crash of looms, urged by weary hands even at this hour, disturbs the silence of the night. And faint rays of light steal out from narrow windows along the street, revealing the exterior of these haunts of misery and want. At every twenty paces, we behold a miserable court, shooting away from this narrow street toward the west, the roofs of its tottering tenements, almost touching overhead. And all is dark, save those faint gleams of light, and all is still save the crash of looms, as they swing to and fro.*

THE HIBERNIA HOSE COMPANY

The Hibernia Engine Company and the Hibernia Hose Company are often confused. Hibernia Engine Company was founded in the city of Philadelphia on January 20, 1752, while Hibernia Hose was founded in Kensington on

Looking north on Cadwalader Street from Master. This block of buildings was destroyed by fire. The Hibernia Hose Company sat roughly where the one-story building is.

November 22, 1842. Hibernia Engine was the first fire company founded in the city and county of Philadelphia. Hibernia Hose was founded by nineteenth-century Irish Catholic immigrants, about a year and a half before the riots broke out in 1844. Hibernia Hose was located on the west side of Cadwalader Street, the first building north of the corner property on the northwest corner of Cadwalader and Master Streets, approximately forty-five feet above Master Street.

A description of the hose company when it marched in the Fireman's Parade of 1843 stated that the Hibernia Hose Company had at least twenty members who wore dark coats and green capes and had a neat appearance. That same year, on September 5, Hibernia Hose asked the commissioners of the District of Kensington for their first semiannual installment of appropriations. The company had originally asked back in 1842 to be put on the list of fire companies that were partially supported by the district when they first organized. A newspaper account of February 10, 1844, about the arrest of four members of Hibernia Hose Company during a fight with Carroll Hose Company over a fire on Cadwalader Street, gave the Hibernia men arrested as John Hinzel, Patrick Campbell, John Mulldon and Bernard McElleore. Hinzel is likely the fellow who lost his carpenter's shop on Cadwalader Street to fire during the riots. Campbell was likely the man arrested for participating in the Kensington Riots.

It is not surprising that a number of the Irish Catholic combatants during the riots of 1844 were stated to be members of the Hibernia Hose Company. Fire companies in the 1830s and 1840s were known to be violent. Much of the initial gunfire in the first day of rioting came from the Hibernia Hose Company's building on Cadwalader Street or from a courtyard directly north of it. The hose company building sat directly west from the Nanny Goat Market, across an empty lot, giving it a prime view of the activities of the nativists' rally and early fighting. Eventually, the riots took their toll on the Hibernia Hose Company, and it was burned down, its carriage destroyed.

THE MASTER STREET SCHOOL

The Master Street School sat on the south side of Master Street, 50 feet west of Second Street. It measured 100 feet wide by about 130 feet deep. The Nanny Goat Market sat just to the northwest of the school, perhaps 210 feet away. The school itself was a three-story brick building, with wood construction, a shingle roof, sod yard and sidewalk paving. It had detached unheated toilets. The building was built in 1832 at the price of $19,009.10, for an average of $1,267.27 per classroom, which gives it in the neighborhood of fifteen classrooms, perhaps five on each floor.

At the time of the riots, Master Street Boys' Grammar (Middle) School had 273 in attendance, and Girls Grammar (Middle) School had 285. The girls' school had as its principal Louisa Bedford, while the boys' school was run by James McClune. There was also an associated primary (elementary) school with a total of 320 boys and girls. The principal was Mary H. Buzby. The Master Street School was the largest school in Kensington, with a total of 1,197 students.

A list of students that were to attend Central High School in January 1844 shows nine students from Kensington, all graduates of the Master Street School. Of these nine, four were Irish Catholics from the Nanny Goat Market neighborhood, the sons of weavers or laborers. Being selected to attend Central High School in 1844 was about equivalent to going to college in most respects. It was a large accomplishment for a working-class family. Only three schools produced more Central High School students at this time.

The next term of July 1844 saw John A. Clark make it into Central High School. He graduated from Master Street School. Clark was the son of Patrick Clark, alderman Hugh Clark's brother. In the 1840s, Master Street was fairly consistent in being in the top three or four schools that had attendees accepted to Central High School. Indeed, it was one of the better schools in Philadelphia.

Master Street School became the focus of the Bible Wars, which led up to the Nativist Riots. This confrontation pitted Protestants and Catholics against each other for what Bible their congregants' children would read in the public schools. Protestants obviously wanted only the King James Bible read, but the Catholics countered with the idea that Catholic students should be allowed to read from the Catholic version of the Bible, or the Douay Bible. It was these troubles over the Bible that inflamed many of the nativists. The sod lot next to the school is where the nativists originally set up their political rally on May 3, 1844, that was broken up by the Irish Catholics. The stage was set up against the side of the school. It was here again that they came on May 6, 1844, only to be broken up again by a rainstorm, leading them to flee to the nearby Nanny Goat Market pavilion, which in turn started the actual combat of the riots. In 1848, the Master Street School had its name changed to the Harrison School. It was vacated in 1891.

Kensington's Third Ward would eventually evolve into Philadelphia's Seventeenth Ward after consolidation of the county into the city in 1854. The area would remain heavily Irish for years after the riots, with its neighboring Eighteenth Ward (Fishtown) staying Protestant. When the 1860 census was taken, it showed that Wards Eleven through Fourteen (Delaware River to Broad Street, Poplar Street down to Vine Street) all had single-digit Irish-born populations. The lowest percentage of Irish born of any ward in Philadelphia was Kensington's Eighteenth Ward. In the Seventeenth Ward of Kensington, where the riots took place, 23.3 percent of the population was Irish born. This ranked the Seventeenth Ward number five in the city for Irish-born population. The frontrunner was the Ninth Ward of Center City, followed by Seventh Ward and then Eighth Ward, both of Center City, and then Fourth Ward (Southwark/Moyamensing) and Kensington's Seventeenth Ward at the fifth spot.

Chapter 3

Early Riots in Kensington

The Riot of 1828

The several generations of Irish Catholics that came to America between the 1790s and 1840s after the failed Irish Rebellion of 1798 would have experienced a Philadelphia that had seen and would see a number of riots among its citizens. No less than three major riots broke out in Kensington alone between the years 1828 and 1843, all of which set the stage for the most violent riots that took place in 1844. In some cases, the same individuals were involved in all of the riots.

According to contemporary newspaper accounts, on Tuesday night, August 12, 1828, a riot took place at a house on Third Street between George Street and today's Girard Avenue. Three persons were arrested and had a hearing before Frederick Wolbert, Esq., and were committed as the instigators of the disturbance. Robert McCoffin, one of the watchmen of the district, was killed while attempting to suppress the riot. A stone was thrown at him, which fractured his skull. Eleazer Hand, another of the watchmen, was wounded in the head by a gunshot. The wound, while dangerous, was not as severe as first thought. Several other persons were seriously injured as well. The police of the District immediately went into action to search for the rioters.

The following night, a number of persons assembled in the neighborhood where the riot had taken place the previous night, and by 10:00 p.m., several hundred had assembled. A flag was hoisted early in the morning at the house of a person named O'Neal, near where the watchman was killed the night before. At about 11:00 p.m., a melee broke out between persons within and those outside the house, which ended in the destruction of the house and the furniture. Those inside the house fired rounds of buckshot, wounding one person severely and another slightly. A person by the name of Nell was found severely beaten with clubs. This may have been O'Neal, mentioned earlier as having a flag raised at his house. The police arrested several of the offenders.

After this second day of rioting, no further disturbances took place in Kensington. The sheriff had called for assistance from the police of the city as well as a detachment of volunteers from the militia. The police and militia patrolled the area, ending the rioting. By August 16, the authorities went home, the disturbance having ended. The commissioners of the Northern Liberties issued a proclamation, offering a reward of $300 for the apprehension and conviction of the murderer of watchman Robert A. McGuffin (also recorded as McCoffin), who was killed on the morning of Tuesday, August 12, 1828.

Historians Scharf and Westcott, who wrote a monumental history of Philadelphia, took a different view of this 1828 riot that was reported in the local Philadelphia newspapers. Scharf and Westcott wrote:

> *August 11, 1828, a riotous disposition was manifested in Kensington amongst some weavers. Stephen Heimer, a watchman, was killed. Two days afterwards another riot took place at the corner of 3rd & George on account of the hanging out of a weaver's banner. Stones and brickbats were fired at the house from which the offensive display was made. Guns were fired, some persons were wounded. The Sheriff called out the posse comitatus, issued his proclamation, and called upon the mayor of the city for help. These occurrences led to the holding of a meeting of native and naturalized citizens of the Northern Liberties and Kensington at the house of John Thoburn being chairman.*

At this meeting, the nativists basically disavowed any native-born Americans taking part in the mayhem, blaming it on the Irish immigrants.

There was no public report on the inquiry of the death of Heimer. Thomas Weldon, James Weldon, George Weldon, James Oliver and John Browne were tried for participation in this riot in December. Apparently, watchman Heimer was not on duty at the time, but he was going along Third Street above Poplar Street making a noise. He went into Weldon's house, which was a tavern or restaurant, to get something to eat or drink. He was requested to be quiet as there was a dying woman in the house. He paid no attention to this request, and the Weldons, with the others, set upon him and beat him so that he died from his injuries. The Weldons were Irish. Heimer, in the quarrel, had called them "bloody Irish transports." These words "repeated excited much indignation among the Irish weavers of the neighborhood, while an opposition to them of Americans quite as strong arose." The second riot was caused by the weavers' taunt in hanging out their banner at the home of O'Neal/Nell. This was the first disturbance in the city or county in which "race prejudice was manifested."

This 1828 riot showed early signs of the nativists versus Irish Catholics mentality. Here, according to Scharf and Wescott, was a Protestant basically challenging the Irish in their own homes, and he suffered terribly. It should also be mentioned that historian Thompson Wescott was a known nativist, thus Scharf and Wescott's writings on the riot of 1828 may be somewhat prejudiced.

Several of the eventual founders of St. Michael's in 1831 were members of a committee formed after the weaver's riot of 1828. A meeting of the native and naturalized citizens of the Northern Liberties and Kensington met at the house of Patrick Murphy on August 18, 1828, to discuss the recent riots and the backlash on the weavers and Irish of Kensington. John Waters was one of the secretaries for the meeting, and Michael Keenan and Henry Crilly were two of the people on the committee that was formed to draft resolutions for the consideration of the meeting. The men at the meeting basically wanted to let the people of Philadelphia know that the troubles caused by a few Irish weavers from Kensington should not mean that the whole of the Irish of Kensington should be blamed. The group made a loud claim that they "absolutely disclaim all participation in the said riotous proceedings and reprobate them as wanton violations of the public peace, and therefore heartily co-operate with any of our fellow citizens in the adoption and execution of measures calculated to prevent the repetition thereof, or to bring to punishment the person or persons therein concerned." Patrick McBride and Bernard McGuire were to represent East Northern Liberties, and Patrick Murphy was one of the two men to represent West Northern Liberties. Henry Crilly was one of the men to represent West Kensington. Murphy, Waters, Keenan, Crilly, McBride and McGuire were all founders of St. Michael's Catholic Church.

RAILROAD RIOTS OF 1840–42

Another riot that took place in Kensington was written about by none other than the famous American writer Edgar Allan Poe. This skirmish, which took place off and on from 1840 to 1842, was called the Railroad Riots. An item attributed to Edgar Allan Poe by Clarence S. Brigham in his *Edgar Allan Poe's Contributions to Alexander's Weekly Messenger* states that Poe wrote about the Kensington Railroad Riots in that publication on March 18, 1840. In an article titled "The Rail Road War," Poe gives us his interpretation of this often overlooked Kensington event:

> *During the last ten days, or thereabouts, the sober inhabitants of the District of Kensington have been all alive with a delightful little war of their own—a nice rough-and-tumble affair—none of your bloodhound business, or Bugaboo and Kickapoo campaigns. The Philadelphia and Trenton Railroad Company had received permission, it seems, from one of our judicial tribunals, to lay their rails in Front street, but could not obtain the consent of the property holders of the region. For some time past the work has been going on, however, with much grumbling and many threats on the part of the Front-streeters, but with no overt act of resistance. On Monday morning, about ten o'clock, matters took the first serious turn. Quite a mob—men, women, and children—surrounded the laborers at the rails; replacing the paving-stones which had been displaced, and otherwise interrupting the work. The sheriff was sent for, arrived about 12, with his posse, and arrested Henry Rowan, John Craydon, and Francis Farley. The arrest of these persons intimidated the crowd for a time, but in the afternoon the riot again commenced. About 4 o'clock Hugh Lemon was arrested, taken before the Mayor, and bound over in the sum of $300* [Hugh Lemon was a large land owner on Front Street].
>
> *On Tuesday and Wednesday the excitement still continued, and a great number of the gentle engaged in the melee. On Thursday the disorders increased. Mr. Naglee was violently assaulted with paving stones discharged from the fair hands of the damsels of Kensington, who also led away in triumph a wagon containing iron rails for the road, the laborers being fairly driven off the ground. Many arrests were made, but with no good effect. In the afternoon the Sheriff and his whole posse were routed, and the rioters, having beaten them off, proceeded to tear up that portion of the road which was the nearest to completion; disengaging not only the rails but the wooden frames, and filling up the excavations with dirt and stones. In*

the meantime placards were posted up calling upon the people to "put down the rail-road nuisance," and addressed especially to the firemen, draymen and carters—who were invited to attend a meeting on Thursday evening, in the Commissioners Hall, Kensington. The meeting was accordingly held, and served, as a matter of course, to inflame the wrath of the mob, who adjourned to the scene of action, and set fire to the timber intended for the road. The Judges of the Court of Quarter Sessions now issued a general warrant, authorizing the Sheriff to command the service of every able-bodied citizen to aid in quelling the disturbances. This officer issued notices accordingly, and gave directions to the whole police force, as well as to all the watchmen, to meet at his office on Friday. But before the time appointed, the Railroad Company had agreed to discontinue the laying of the rails until the decision of the Supreme Court could be obtained. An announcement of the Company's submission was duly made by the Sheriff to the mob, who first raised an uproarious shout of triumph, and then dispersed in high glee. Thus ended the great rail-road war.

While Poe tells us the "great rail-road war" ended, in fact, it dragged out until June 1842. According to historian Michael Feldberg, there were outbursts at least "four different times between March 2, 1840 and February 3, 1841."

The residents along Front Street, between Girard and Montgomery, refused to allow the construction of a railroad down the middle of their street. This area ran through the eastern edge of West Kensington, the Irish Catholic neighborhood of St. Michael's parish, scene of the Nativist Riots in 1844. The ashes and sparks of the railroad created a hazardous environment to wooden homes and stores, not to mention the danger to the neighborhood children. There was also the disruption of cross-street traffic to the local draymen and carters. Every time the railroad's workmen showed up, they were driven off. Several of the men arrested had Irish-sounding surnames: Calvin Higgins, Henry Rowan, John Craydon, John Scott, Wesley Flavel, Francis Farley, John Ford, Hugh Lemon, James McMichael, William Sillery, Jacob Friedley and Samuel McCormick. All of those arrested were held on bail between $1,500 and $2,500. Even a Mr. Paynter, one of the commissioners of the District of Kensington, was arrested and charged with participating in the riot. Jacob Albright, the brother of Peter Albright, who figured prominently for the nativists in the Kensington Riots of 1844, was one of those who acted as a constable, helping to arrest the railroad rioters. Flavel would later be arrested in 1844 for murdering his niece and shooting his wife.

In late July 1840, Emery's Tavern at Front and Phoenix (Thompson), the sheriff's posse's headquarters, was torched and burnt down. According to the *National Gazette* of August 1, 1840, the "value of the building destroyed by the riots was about $8,000. This estimate did not include the personal loss of Mr. Emery, the landlord, in furniture, stock, &c., probably from $2,000 to $3,000. Also, there was a box which contained Emery's savings for many years under his bed, this box was taken from under the bed and carried off before the fire was much under way. When Mr. Emery found that his all was lost—he was overcome by his feelings, and conducted out with difficulty by his friends—amid the yells of those outside, who for some time had prevented their escape, even while the house was burning."

According to Feldberg, the building of the railroad became a struggle between "Popular Rights" and "Monopoly Capitalism," and this time popular rights won out. The railroad gave up, and the state legislature gave in: the railroad was not built. Ironically enough, eighty years later, Southeastern Pennsylvania Transportation Authority's (SEPTA) Frankford Elevated Train, the "El," was built down the middle of Front Street. The Railroad Riots actually saw Irish Catholics and Protestants fighting together on the same side.

THE WEAVERS' RIOT OF 1843

In January 1843, rioting took place in Kensington among the weavers. This predated the Nativist Riots by only sixteen months. The riot started in the western part of Moyamensing on Monday, January 9, and lasted about three days. About three hundred journeymen weavers had long been complaining of low wages and went on strike. Finding out that there were weavers working below scale, they gathered to assault these weavers' homes, both in Kensington and Moyamensing. They paraded in the streets and entered the houses of the weavers, tore their chains from the looms and, in some instances, destroyed other property and beat up the inhabitants of the houses. At one house on McDuffie Street, near the Schuylkill, occupied by a man named Sandy McFarlane, a musket was pointed at the rioters but not fired. Enraged, the rioters broke open his door and destroyed everything they could get their hands on. One of the bosses showed up and quarreled with the rioters for attacking his workers and destroying his material. The result was that the boss was severely beaten and narrowly escaped with his life. A number of rioters carried firearms and other weapons. The mob was led mostly by men from the upper districts of Kensington and Northern Liberties, who did most of the damage. A strong presence of police in the southwest part of the city of Philadelphia prevented the violence from spreading across the borders and into the city.

Contemporary newspapers reported on the rioting. From Philadelphia's *North American* of January 10–14, 1843, we find the following accounts. On Monday afternoon, January 9, 1843, in Kensington, a "party of weavers went into Hopkins Court and into the dwellings of several houses and tore from various looms a quantity of material and destroyed it." The next day, about dark, they entered "the house of a weaver on the Germantown Road above the junction of Third Street, where they also destroyed some chain. They tore out some material from a loom, broke the loom and other property, kicked the man's wife and trampled one of his children on the ground. They dragged about the streets the material from the loom and afterward cut it to pieces." In Moyamensing, "a party of them, with some persons representing the manufacturers, had a meeting" at the Nanny Goat Market and agreed to suspend further hostilities until another meeting should be held, when "an understanding might be affected." It was said at that time that nearly all the weavers had work, but some "dissatisfied spirits, for some reason, are nevertheless determined to commit these outrages."

On Wednesday, January 11, the same paper reported:

> *A riot took place in Kensington at the Nanny Goat Market, north end, near Mud Lane. Rioters were armed with clubs, stones and fire arms. The Sheriff organized a posse of two to three hundred and proceeded to the Market House from Commissioner's Hall* [Frankford and Master]. *On approaching the mob, the posse was attacked viciously by a shower of stones and several pieces of fire arms were discharged. A number of the posse were struck and knocked down and in a moment were dispersed by the rioters. The Sheriff received several blows and was considerably injured. Some eight to ten persons were arrested and put into the Northern Liberties watch-house. Up to eleven o'clock at night the rioters maintained the mastery and threatened vengeance.*

By week's end, it was reported that the sheriff was suffering from injuries received the previous night (Thursday) in his attempt to disperse the rioters in Kensington:

We are happy to state, however that he is not seriously hurt and will soon be able to return to his official duties. One of the men who struck him is identified and under arrest. It is quite time that the severest legal punishments should make an example for the men who periodically disturb the peace of the city and disgrace its name by outrages upon persons and property.

On Thursday morning, a company of milita volunteers arrived on the scene in Kensington, and several arrests were made based on warrants issued by Alderman Clark. During the afternoon, a large crowd assembled in the vicinity of the riots. Several fights took place, which resulted in nothing serious. The police officer of the district, under the order of the market committee, repaired to the market in Master Street (Nanny Goat Market) with a carter to take the brickbats away, which had been gathered the preceding day and night. After he had got them into the cart, he was attacked, with the carter driven from the area and the bricks thrown back again. Alderman Clark received an anonymous letter stating that the rioters had "pledged themselves under oath, to burn his house and do him personal violence."

The rioters that were arrested on Wednesday night had a hearing on Thursday afternoon before Mayor Scott, and eight of them were committed: William Costello, in default of $2,000; Patrick McVay, $2,500; Barney McAleer, $2,000; James Welsh, $2,500; Edward Develin, $2,000; John McVay, $5,000; Thomas McConroy, $2,000; and Archibald Develin, $5,000. Archibald Develin was the man who attacked the sheriff.

On Friday, January 13, the National Guard was finally called out and stationed at the armory. They were the volunteers of the First Brigade under the command of Brigadier General George Cadwalader, who would later see action during the 1844 rioting. A large police force was also stationed at Kensington's Commissioner's Hall under William Rawle, acting for the sheriff. However, at an early hour the crowd dispersed, and by 10:00 p.m., it was again quiet.

The rioting at the Nanny Goat Market and the Irishmen arrested would seem to beckon the coming days of the Nativist Riots. Some of the same men arrested (McVay, McAleer, Develin) would also be arrested in May 1844, and the scene of the rioting was the same location as the May 1844 riots when the market house was burned down. Overall, Kensington's Irish had plenty of experience when it came to armed conflict. If it wasn't fighting the English and the Protestants back home in Ireland, it was fighting in the streets of Kensington in America.

Philadelphia politicians must have felt that all the riots in the city and county were not good for attracting business or residents. Earlier, on May 31, 1841, the assembly passed an ordinance that stated, "In all cases where any dwelling house or other building or property real or personal, has been or shall be destroyed within the county of Philadelphia, in consequence of any mob or riot, it shall be lawful for the person or persons interested in, and owning such property, to bring suit against the said county where such property was situated by reason of destruction thereof, and the amount which shall be recovered in said action shall be paid out of the county treasury, on warrants drawn by the Commissioners thereof, who are hereby required to draw the same as soon as said damages are finally fixed and ascertained." Of course, if the party was involved in the rioting, they had no cause to file a suit for damages. This ordinance would come into play for the Irish Catholics of Kensington and St. Michael's and St. Augustine's Churches when they had their property destroyed by the nativist mobs in May 1844.

CHAPTER 4

THE FOUNDING OF THE NATIVIST PARTY

The earliest nativist meeting in Philadelphia took place in Germantown at Mullen's Railroad House (Germantown Road and Price Street) on August 31, 1837, when it was decided to form an organization in the township to maintain native rights, which, it was contended, were being menaced by foreigners. At another meeting on September 7, 1837, a constitution was adopted and the name that was approved was the "Native American Association of the United States in the Township of Germantown." The officers chosen were: Jonathan Wolf, president; Samuel Butcher, vice-president; Dr. Thomas F. Betton, corresponding secretary; Edward Bockius, recording secretary; and Daniel E. Topham, treasurer.

Soon after the official founding of the Native American group, a newspaper account mentioned that there was an organization of an association at Germantown, under the title of "Native Americans." It was charged that this group was associated with the Whigs. The *Germantown Telegraph* published the proceedings of this meeting, and it was found that all the men who were elected to officers were Van Buren men (Democrats), not Whigs. It is odd that these early nativists were Van Buren men, since Van Buren, while the first American-born president (his predecessors were born as British subjects), grew up speaking Dutch as his first language. This same article stated that a communication denouncing the organization of this association was published in a local "morning paper" a "day or two since." The nativists would seem to be attacked even before they got going, as the Whigs did not want to be associated with them at this point in history.

The president of this original nativist group was Jonathan Wolf (1809–1878), a Methodist and local politician in Germantown, holding various offices over his career, from post master to running for Congress in his district on the Democratic ticket. "Captain Wolf," as he was titled, was presented a handsome sword in July 1837, and there was also a new troop of Light Cavalry to be organized in Germantown at this very time, to be called the "Germantown Troop." Perhaps a coincidence, but it would look like the men of Germantown were organizing for battle, both politically and in the street.

However, the Germantowners seem to have been ahead of their time, as the loud noise of 1837 fizzled out and the cry of the Native Americans was silenced until 1843, when, after years of a prolonged economic depression brought on by the bad times of the Panic of 1837, the ugly head of nativism rose again. Founded in New York City, the American Republican Party (aka Native Americans, or simply nativists) started out as a minor party but in 1844 carried the municipal elections in New York City and Philadelphia. The party expanded widely and by July 1845 held a national convention. The members would continue to be a presence in American politics until the mid-1850s, when they finally splintered, with many (the antislavery element) merging with the new Republican Party of Abraham Lincoln.

In 1838, the new Pennsylvania constitution gave the vote to all white men twenty-one years and older, giving many new immigrants the right to vote. In 1841, the mayor of Philadelphia became an elected position, instead of being appointed by council, and thus these newly franchised immigrants could possibly sway the election for the mayor. With the influx of Irish Catholics into Philadelphia and especially their quick attraction to politics, the nativists' blood began to boil. According to historian J. Matthew Gallam, Philadelphia County at this time pitted Whigs against Democrats, with the Whigs controlling the city proper and the Democrats controlling the surrounding districts (such as Kensington), where many Irish Catholics were moving. The new American Republican Party would tend to draw mostly from the Whigs, although a number of Democrats also joined their ranks, out of their hatred of the Irish and the Catholic Church.

Nativist sympathies were very high in Kensington both before and after the riots of 1844. Kensington was an old district, settled in the 1730s, and included among its citizens many "native"-born men whose families fought in the American Revolution. In the elections held in October 1844, just after the riots, all six seats that were up for grabs on the board of commissioners for the District of Kensington were filled with nativist candidates (American

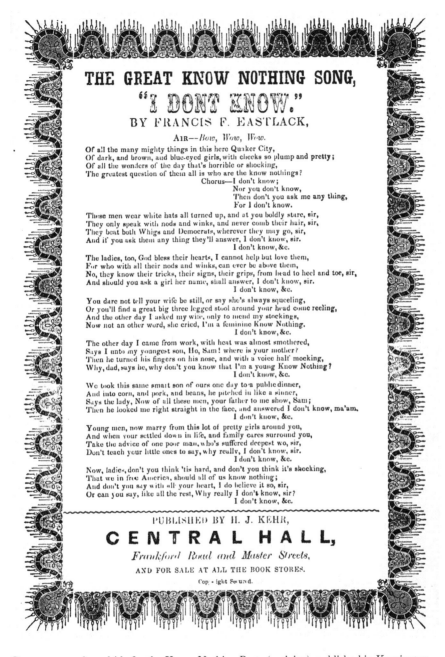

Contemporary broadside for the Know-Nothing Party (nativists), published in Kensington, at Frankford and Master, at Central Hall.

Republican Party): Charles Delany (First Ward, serving three years), Solomon Wagner (Third Ward), Michael Collar (Fifth Ward), Samuel T. Bodine (Second Ward), Jacob Teese (Fourth Ward) and John H. Hammitt (First Ward, serving three years). With obvious signs of a growing political movement, it was then left to the Protestant churches to come into the nativist fold, which they willingly did.

The American Protestant Association and the Bible Wars

The state legislature of Pennsylvania enacted a law in 1838 that stated that the King James Bible would be a mandatory textbook in the public schools of Pennsylvania. For children of Catholics, this meant that they would be subject to religious teachings that were contrary to their religious beliefs. For Catholic children, there was no school choice in 1838, as the parochial school system was not yet established. For the most part, Catholics did not make much of a fuss about this new regulation, as they were mainly immigrant Irish recently arrived in a foreign country. However, Catholic bishops did see it as a problem and acted accordingly. New York's Bishop John Hughes (1797–1864) made it his fight to attack this law, which was aimed primarily at his people. Philadelphia's Bishop Patrick Kendrick (1796–1863) followed up Bishop Hughes's lead and advocated for the Catholics of Philadelphia to read their own Bible. In a letter of 1842, Bishop Hughes wrote to the Philadelphia school directors, requesting that Catholic children be excused from reading the King James Bible. The school board, basically a Protestant body, responded that Catholics could be excused from reading the King James Bible, but they would have to substitute it with another Bible, one that would not be permitted to have notes or commentary. Since the Catholic Douay Bible did contain notes and commentary, the school board was basically telling the bishop "no," because the Douay Bible was not going to be permitted in the public schools. Bishop Kenrick did not pursue the matter further, but the torch had been lit and the Protestant ministers of Philadelphia started lining up to flame the fire.

But the details of the incident were lost in the rumor mill. Surveyor Benjamin Moore (1784–1864), of North Second Street, a fanatical Protestant said to be from a local Kensington Methodist Church, began whipping up hysteria. This man has been misidentified in history as Henry Moore. Benjamin Moore and others set up a series of rallies to "save the Bible."

Alderman Hugh Clark's (1796–1862) tombstone (left), St. Michael's Cemetery. He was one of the founders of St. Michael's Church, and his house was sacked during the riots.

Locally, in Kensington, in late February 1844, Moore, a newly elected director on the school board (along with Irish Catholic Hugh Clark) for the District of Kensington, mistakenly reported to his Methodist congregation in Kensington that Clark ordered Louisa Bedford, the principal at the Master Street School, not to read the Bible in her classroom. However, Clark never told Bedford to stop reading the Bible; rather, he suggested it might be wise to suspend the reading until the controversy could be worked out. He left the actual decision up to Bedford, as she was the principal of the girls' school. Bedford, a resident of the Northern Liberties, was not a newcomer to Kensington. She had been working at the Master Street School since 1834 and remained there until at least 1855. She had been the principal of the girls' school since 1842. Clark felt that if reading or not reading the Bible was causing disruption in her class, then Bedford should take some sort of action to remedy the situation. It was Bedford, and not Clark, who suspended the

Bible reading. However, the damage was done. Moore and his misinformed message were enough to arouse the Protestants of Kensington, who really did not need much awakening, what with many Protestant ministers already making a call to arms. As the Protestants saw it, the Church of Rome was attempting to take over America by attempting to install its Bible in the public schools. To the Protestant ministers of Philadelphia, this was enough for them to organize to fight the Church of Rome.

The American Protestant Association (APA) was formed in Philadelphia in 1842, the same year as Bishop Kenrick's letter to the school board. Its founders, all Protestant ministers at Philadelphia churches, were frightened at the prospect of the spread of Roman Catholicism in the United States. Their opinions of the Catholic Church were that it was "subversive of civil and religious liberty." The ministers accordingly formed an association to further their Protestant interests, which were to educate their congregations about the differences between Protestantism and Catholicism, or what they called "Popery." They thought to do this by encouraging a thorough study of the Bible—the King James Bible, for sure. The association set out to welcome members from all Protestant denominations. One piece of its propaganda machine was a quarterly journal, which basically consisted of anti-Catholic sermons and "Popery" articles denouncing the Catholic church and the Pope in every imaginable way. The APA in essence became the theological arm of the nativist movement. While the American Republican Party worked the political halls of the city and county to secure its interests by law, the APA worked the pulpits of churches throughout Philadelphia and beyond, helping to agitate the mobs, which would eventually lead to the killings and church burnings of the Nativist Riots of 1844.

The twenty-six clergymen who founded the APA consisted of ministers from Presbyterian, Episcopalian, Baptist, Methodist, Dutch Reformed, Lutheran and Moravian churches. The leaders of the APA were, as one might expect, the Presbyterians, with at least seven ministers registered among the original twenty-six founders. Of the eighty-one different ministers who attended the first three meetings of the newly formed group, at least twenty-seven of them were Presbyterians. A total of ninety-four ministers signed their names to the newly written APA's constitution, including some fairly well-known and respected ministers both citywide and in Kensington, including Reverend H.A. Boardman, Reverend John S. Inskip and Reverend Albert Helffenstein Jr. The original board of directors consisted of: Reverend E.F. Backus, president; Reverend Stephen H. Tyng, D.D., vice-president; Reverend John Kennaday, vice-president; Reverend George B. Ide, vice-president; Reverend Henry A.

Reverend John S. Inskip (1816–1884), of Kensington's "Old Brick Church," gave a speech at the nativist rally in March 1844, which helped flame the anger of the nativists.

Boardman, corresponding secretary; Reverend William W. Spear, recording secretary; and Mr. A.H. Julian, treasurer. Philadelphia's ministers were not the only bigots in America, as the famed Reverend Lyman Beecher, considered an enlightened minister given his relationship to Harriet Beecher Stowe, argued that Catholic immigration was a danger to American Republicanism. Another well-known personality who sided with the nativists was Samuel F.B. Morse, the inventor of Morse code, who agreed with Beecher.

One of the best (or worst) summations of the founding of the APS is included in a contemporary pamphlet published just after the Nativist Riots called *The Truth Unveiled*, where the organization was described as follows:

> *The formation of such a society was regarded by all, who dared to think upon matters with reference to their results, as the war-cry for Protestants to take the field against Catholics; for the summons to renew their battle, in which Christian was to be seen contending with Christian, and the very altars of God were to be desecrated by their priests; who instead of bringing upon them the offering of broken hearts and contrite spirits, cast there the sharpened sword without its scabbard, the weapon for bloody strife, that were dedicated to the work of religious or rather sectarian persecution.*

Thus, Sunday after Sunday, Protestant ministers went to work on their congregations, painting the Catholic Church in general and Irish Catholics in particular as the latest evil confronting America's Constitution. With the ministers hammering from the pulpit and the American Republicans hammering from the soapbox, it was no wonder that all the finger pointing and vitriol would eventually lead to the worst rioting that was ever seen in the history of Philadelphia.

Founding of the Nativist Party in West Kensington

In December 1843, a meeting was convened at a hall on the Ridge Road (Avenue) in the district of Spring Garden, an area bordering the then city of Philadelphia's northwest. Out of this meeting was formed the "American Republican Association of the Second Ward, Spring Garden."

Meetings were regularly held at a hall known as the Sign of the Ball on Ridge Road. Sign of the Ball was so named due to the fact that a ball was hung in front of the building. The ball was illuminated on the evenings of the association's meetings. This ball was shot up on occasion, and, of course, the Irish Catholics were blamed for these actions.

In January 1844, another association of American Republicans was formed in Locust Ward, within the City of Philadelphia, and soon after, associations were formed in North Mulberry and Cedar Wards, also in Philadelphia. After several months, associations were formed in almost every ward throughout the city and county of Philadelphia, except for West Kensington. Kensington at this time was divided into "East" and "West," for governmental purposes. The dividing line was Frankford Road.

The "Declaration of Principles" that was approved by these early American Republican Associations was:

1. *Naturalization laws should be altered to require all foreigners a residence of 21 years before granting them the privilege of the elective franchise* [voting and holding office].
2. *The Bible* [King James] *should be used in all public schools as a reading book.*
3. *Opposed to a union of church and state in any form.*
4. *Only native Americans should be appointed to office, to legislate, administer, or execute the laws of their own country.*

"Freedom to the Americans," a nativist flag, showing a monument to those nativists who died during the Kensington Riot of May 1844.

No matter what name they used—American Republicans, Native Americans, nativists or, later, the Know-Nothings—their ideology was still the same: disenfranchise the Irish Catholics; keep the Irish in their place as second-class citizens, if indeed they were to be citizens at all; and by all means, do not allow the Catholic Church to advance in America.

A very large meeting concerning the reading of the Bible in public schools was held by nativists at the Commissioner's Hall in Kensington (southeast corner Frankford and Master) on March 4, 1844 (apparently another meeting had been held the previous Monday, February 26, 1844, and this March 4 meeting was a continuation).

As its presiding officer, George App, Esq., called the meeting to order. Thomas J. Taylor and H.A. Salters assisted. It was estimated that 2,500 people were present. The hall held not even half the number of people who showed up.

E.D. Tarr, Esq., spoke first, saying, "We have come to this meeting as American Christians, and assert our rights as Americans." Tarr went on to fire up the audience, finally resolving that any district teachers be allowed to read from the Bible as they see fit, without notes or commentary, which would exclude the Catholic Bible, as it had notes and commentary.

H.A. Salters was the next to speak. At the previous meeting he had been on the committee that was appointed to draft resolutions, a preamble, etc. He made it known that the Board of School Commissioners should elect no man that would be against the reading of the Holy Bible in schools. This resolution was unanimously adopted.

Peter Rambo next offered a resolution to let the school board know that in the Tenth District (Kensington), the reading of the Bible had been left up to the teachers; however, he thought it should be up to the board.

Thomas J. Taylor was next to speak. He agreed with Rambo but thought it needed to go further, that a committee of twenty should be formed, four from each of the districts' five wards. The committee would draw up a petition to the state legislature, putting into the hands of the school board directors the full power of what was to be read in the classrooms and the directors to be elected in the spring elections. The resolution got unanimous support.

After Taylor came the Reverend Barg and the Reverend Inskip. Inskip, a former minister at Kensington Methodist Episcopal "Old Brick" Church, offered the following resolution: he viewed the efforts of the Roman Catholics trying to read their own Bible in school as an attempt to abolish the Bible altogether from the schools. He felt that it was a sure indication that the Church of Rome continued to grasp after unauthorized power and designed to take from people their rights. Inskip went on to say, "We here pledge our property, our influence, our prayers, our lives and our sacred honor" to guard these rights. It seemed Inskip was saying that people needed to be willing to put their lives on the line to fight the Roman Catholics. Reverend Inskip would later become a prominent leader of the Methodist Holiness Movement in America.

Henry Sitler, a member of the American Republican Association of New York, spoke next on the history of the doings of the Catholic church of Bishop Hughes in New York. Reverend Ketchum and Abraham P. Eyre, Esq., also spoke. Eyre was from a prominent family of Kensington shipbuilders who dated back to the American Revolution and was at present a commissioner for the District of Kensington.

John Painter spoke next, relating his conversations with Ms. Bedford, the public school principal at Master Street School, concerning the conversations she had with Alderman Hugh Clark and the reading of the Bible.

Mr. Tarr then made a resolution to have Painter request a copy of the school board proceedings concerning Clarke and Bedford. Reverend

Webster and H.A. Salters then addressed the meeting and resolved to pledge themselves individually and collectively to oppose the reelection of anyone on the school board who voted for Hugh Clark (an Irish Catholic) for the school district or any other office. They also encouraged the crowd to support the *North American* and the *Daily Sun*, two nativist newspapers.

On a motion by George J. Hamilton, the meeting was adjourned to meet again the next Monday (March 11, 1844) at the statehouse yard (Independence Hall). Several of the men (H.A. Salters, George J. Hamilton, Abraham P. Eyres, Reverend Inskip) at this meeting were associated with Kensington Methodist Episcopal Church and the Kensington Soup Society, a local charitable group, founded by Kensington's Protestants.

At this time, the local nativists of Kensington's Third Ward decided to form an American Republican Association in their area and called for a meeting at the house of John Gee on May 1, 1844. Gee lived on Second Street, about half way between Phoenix (Thompson) and Jefferson Streets, or almost directly across the street from St. Michael's Catholic Church. It was no accident that the nativists would schedule their first meeting right in the heart of Kensington's Irish Catholic community and at the doorstep of their church. When Gee began to receive threats that his house or any other house in the area would be burned down if they sponsored a nativist meeting, Gee worried for his property and cancelled the meeting. Gee's cancelling forced the nativists to meet in the adjoining Second Ward of Kensington. Other meetings for the Third Ward had also been held in the Second Ward, as the Third Ward was dominated by Irish Catholics and they would not have anti–Irish Catholic speeches spewed in their neighborhood.

While invitations were sent out to various leaders of the party, those leaders balked at having to have to speak in the Second Ward for the Third Ward and thus would not address the meetings unless they were held in their proper place. Because of this, the Third Ward Association placed an advertisement in the *Native American* on May 2 and 3, 1844:

> *A Meeting of the Native Born Citizens of the Third Ward, Kensington, was held on Monday evening, the 29th ult. After electing officers, they adjourned to meet in mass meeting on Friday afternoon, May 3, at 6 o'clock, at the corner of Second and Master streets. All friendly to the cause are invited to attend. Wm. Craig, Prest. John McManus, Sec'y.*

THE ASSAULT ON THE NATIVIST MEETING
OF MAY 3, 1844

The meeting that was held on May 3 at the southwest corner of Second and Master Streets had the purpose of considering the expediency of a proposed alteration of the laws of the United States, in reference to the naturalization of foreigners, and promoting the ends and objects of the association known as the Native American Party. This nativist meeting was to be held on an empty lot, measuring 100 by 150 feet, next to the Master Street Public School, site of the "Bible Wars" between Alderman Clark and the teachers of the district. The school was located on Master Street, about midway between Second and Washington (American) Streets and about seventy yards east of the Nanny Goat Market (Washington Market).

Having the meeting held in an empty lot alleviated the American Republicans' worry that a man's house would be destroyed by the Irish Catholics if he held a meeting. In a way, the nativists having a rally in West Kensington at that time would be akin to the Ku Klux Klan having a rally in the middle of North Philadelphia today. The African Americans in North Philly wouldn't stand for a Klan rally, and Kensington's Irish Catholics in 1844 would not accept the nativists either. It was a bad idea, a recipe for disaster, but politics and prejudice being what they were, the meeting took place on May 3, 1844.

A littler earlier, in April 1844, just days before the May 3 meeting, local newspapers reported the "Weavers" of Kensington were in an uproar again. One man was pulled from his house, his loom and textile work destroyed and he was "rode through the area on an inch board." His crime: he dared to take home weaving work below the fixed rate. The paper reported that there was every indication that there might be a larger riot soon. The sheriff was asked for protection.

On May 2, the day before the scheduled nativist meeting in Kensington, Lewis C. Levin, one of the leaders of the nativists, was attacked at Fourth and Lombard Streets by a fellow named John Manderfield. Levin was walking down the street with his wife and two children. He lived nearby. Manderfield, coming up behind Levin, said some insulting remarks regarding Levin being a nativist. Levin wheeled around and hit Manderfield, knocking him to the ground. Manderfield got up and made a run at Levin, hitting him on the neck. Levin in turn gave Manderfield several blows to the head, cutting him severely. Several others nearby approached to help Manderfield, but Captain R.F. Stockton of the United States Navy, who lived nearby, happened by in his carriage and prevented further attacks on Levin. The nativist newspaper *North American* stated that it appeared to be a premeditated attack on Levin.

Lewis Charles Levin was born November 10, 1808, at Charleston, South Carolina. He was one of the main leaders of the nativist movement. Oddly enough, he was the son of Jewish parents, but he later converted to Christianity and became a Methodist Street preacher, attorney and newspaper editor.

He graduated from South Carolina College (later to become the University of South Carolina) in 1828. It is said that he briefly taught school in Woodville, Mississippi, but left town after being wounded in a duel. His second in the duel was said to have been Jefferson Davis, the future president of the Southern Confederacy. After leaving Mississippi, Levin read and practiced law in Maryland, Louisiana and Kentucky before moving to Philadelphia by 1838.

While in Philadelphia, Levin became active in the Temperance Movement, founding and editing a journal called the *Temperance Advocate*. He gave numerous speeches and lectures on the evils of alcohol and became quite prominent in the movement.

Along with temperance issues, Levin became active against what he saw as the gaining strength of Catholic political power due to the arrival of many Irish Catholics. He became quite prominent in the nativist movement as well, becoming one of the founders of the Nativist Party in the 1840s. He was editor of the *Native American* and the *Dailey Sun*, two anti-Catholic newspapers of Philadelphia at that time.

Levin became the spokesman for nativists. At both the Kensington Riots in May 1844 and the Southwark Riots of July 1844, Levin gave speeches that led to public disorder in those neighborhoods, resulting in mass rioting, death and destruction. Levin and his colleague Samuel R. Kramer, publisher of the *Native American*, were arrested and fined for "exciting to riot and treason."

Levin's popularity among the ignorant class helped propel him to be elected to the United States Congress, where he served three terms for Pennsylvania's First District from 1845 to 1851. As support for the nativist movement began to decline in the 1850s, Levin lost his bid for a fourth congressional term. Even though he no longer practiced Judaism and considered himself a Christian, Levin is technically called the first Jewish congressman in American history.

While Levin lost his congressional seat, he continued to campaign for nativist and Know-Nothing causes. In 1856, he organized a meeting to start a movement against the presidential campaign of John Fremont. The meeting, held at National Hall (Independence Hall), broke up in a disturbance, with Levin being ejected from the platform. This was the last public appearance that he made.

His mind had become so crazed that friends feared he was going insane, which he did. He became so deranged that he was picked up by the police in September 1856 and committed to the Pennsylvania Hospital for the Insane, where he died of "insanity" on March 14, 1860. He was buried in Laurel Hill Cemetery. His death was covered in the national press.

Even after death, controversy still surrounded Levin. Money to build a monument for him at Laurel Hill Cemetery disappeared, and it wouldn't be until recent times that a plaque with his name would be set and his monument finished. After Levin's death, his wife, Julia, and at least one of his daughters (Thomassina or Louisa) converted to Catholicism. At the time of the Kensington Riots, Levin lived on South Fourth Street in Center City, later moving to South Eleventh Street, below Spruce Street, his address when he was committed to the insane asylum.

The May 3 meeting assembled at the empty lot at Second and Master Streets at about 4:00 p.m. Depending on who you believe, the crowd was estimated to be between one hundred and three hundred people, including a large number of noisy boys, the greater portion of whom were foreign born (Irish Catholics) and residents of the ward who were opposed to the object of the meeting. Along with the Irish Catholics, the rest of the crowd were made up of various nativists from around the city, mostly men and boys from Kensington, Northern Liberties, Spring Garden, Southwark and Moyamensing.

Samuel R. Kramer, the editor of the *Native American*, was called for and immediately appeared to address the meeting. It was evident rather quickly that there was displeasure among the Irish Catholics as to Kramer's remarks. Individuals kept pouring in to the meeting from various parts of the neighborhood. He had not gotten far in his speech when he was "assailed with threats of violence and clubs were seen brandishing in the air." Patrick Lafferty was the Irish Catholic that shouted down Kramer for claiming immigrants wanted to change the Constitution. Lafferty screamed out that he was an immigrant, now naturalized, and that he supported the Constitution. Joanna Maloy, who would later testify at the riot trials, stated that the meeting on May 3 was broken up because the speaker mentioned there was a group of "Germans and Irish who wanted to get the Constitution of the United States into their own hands, and sell the country to a foreign power." Someone from the meeting yelled, "That is the Pope, to hell with him." At this point, Lafferty called the speaker a liar and said he himself was an Irishman and a naturalized citizen and supported the Constitution.

Kramer never got to finish his speech. The May 3 meeting was finally broken up with further haranguing from the audience's Irish Catholics, as well as a number of rocks starting to be thrown. Eventually, a rush was made toward the stage, chasing the speaker from the rostrum. The Irish Catholic mob then attacked the stage itself. The stage had been erected up against the Master Street School's fence. The mob pulled the stage's boards apart and scattered them around the lot. The nativists, outnumbered, scattered and were chased by the Catholic mob for a short distance. No one was reported to have been physically hurt. Thomas Walls gathered up the boards from the stage and made a celebratory bonfire of them. John Daley, John Donnelly, Patrick Lafferty, Thomas McWilliams, John O'Neill, James Sherry, Hugh Flanagan and Thomas Walls would all be arrested later and charged with rioting for breaking up this meeting. Round one went to the Irish Catholics.

The nativists, although angered that their freedom of assembly and free speech rights were trounced on, did not offer any resistance, which was good for them because they were vastly outnumbered. Rather, they decided to reconvene their meeting that night at another location, reorganizing the meeting at the George Fox Temperance Hall at Second Street and Germantown Road. William Craig served as the chairman and John McManus as secretary. At this occasion, they resolved to carry out their meeting again at Second and Master Streets in Kensington on the following Monday, May 6, 1844, at 4:00 p.m. One would think that a break over the weekend would help to cool the heads of the combatants, but no such luck was in store. The fighting would become worse, much worse than anyone could have imagined.

CHAPTER 5

MONDAY, MAY 6, 1844

THE FIRST DAY OF RIOTING

Note: The accounts of the three days of riots contained in these next three chapters are taken mainly from contemporary newspaper reports and the testimony of eyewitnesses during the riot court trials.

RECONVENING AND BREAKUP OF THE MAY 6 MEETING

The first day of rioting started in Kensington on May 6, 1844. In all, the riot lasted three days. During each of the three days, the nativists would rally downtown with their supporters and march back in numbers to Kensington to fight again. Monday, May 6, 1844, was the day that the nativists vowed to continue their meeting at Second and Master Street, the meeting that was broken up by an assault of the Irish Catholics on May 3. For this second attempt at the meeting in Kensington, some of the nativists came armed and, in all likelihood, were hoping for a conflict.

The nativist papers advertised that the meeting for May 6 was to convene at 4:00 p.m., and all were encouraged to attend. The people responded with upward of four thousand in attendance. While this figure may have been exaggerated, there was certainly many more then the one to three hundred that showed up on May 3.

Staging was again erected against the Master Street School's fence and an American flag raised over it. Three hearty cheers were given, and the

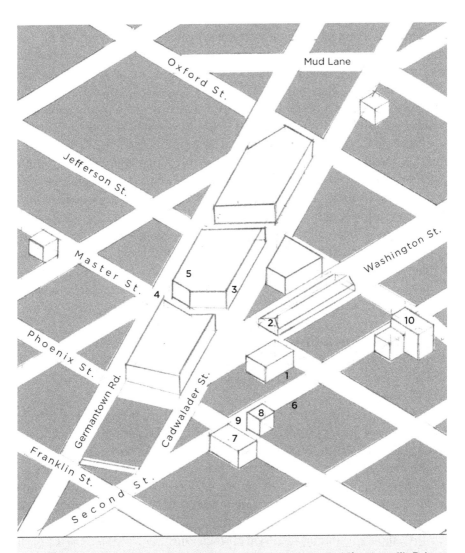

KENSINGTON RIOTS ON DAY ONE, MAY 6, 1844. Nativists met at the stage (1). Rain forced them to the Nanny Goat Market (2). Rocks thrown at Hibernia Hose (3). Catholics regrouped with stones, bricks and guns. Shiffler & Cox were shot (4). Houses of John Lafferty, widow Brady, Michael Quinn and John Brown were battered with missiles and damaged, breaking doors and windows (5). Mob broke into houses (6) destroying furniture and demolishing the windows so the occupants fled. Seminary / former Nunnery (7) was attacked but the mob were dispersed by Catholics atop Corr's Temperance grocery (8) who fired a volley of ball and buckshot. Nathan Ramsay and William Wright were shot and killed (9). Others wounded. Catholics ran to St. Michael's (10) to protect it from rumors of arson.

A bird's-eye view of the first day of the Kensington Riots on May 6, 1844, with legend showing events and actions during the afternoon and evening. *Courtesy Torben Jenk.*

meeting was organized by the secretary reading the proceedings of the former meeting. Samuel R. Kramer was the first speaker called to the stage. He gave the same speech that he was unable to finish on May 3. Next in line was Colonel Peter Sken Smith. Like Lewis C. Levin, Smith was one of the nativist leaders. A colonel in the militia, an editor and a temperance lecturer, Smith turned his talents to American Republican organizing. Smith's father was Peter Smith, the wealthy partner of John Jacob Astor. The elder Smith made a fortune in land speculation. Like his father, the younger Smith started out quite successful. Around 1830, he went to St. Augustine and became one of Florida's first promoters. He became the largest developer in St. Augustine but then came the Panic of 1837, and Smith lost his fortune almost overnight. He fled Florida, one step ahead of the sheriff and his creditors. Moving to Philadelphia, Smith became involved in the temperance and nativist movements. Eventually, like Levin, he went insane, dying in 1858. Oddly enough, Smith, while showing great prejudice against Irish Catholics, was the brother of Garrit Smith, the famed abolitionist and social reformer.

Also on the stage was Reverend John Perry (printer of the *Awful Riots* book and a Protestant minister) and William R. Craig, the chairman of the meeting. Craig invited any of the Irish Catholics to come up to the stage to have a dialogue on the issues being discussed. No Irishman accepted his offer.

At about 4:45 p.m., while Colonel Smith was speaking, an Irish Catholic by the name of John O'Neill, a carter, drove a cart of dirt onto the lot about ten feet below Master, through the densest part of the meeting. There was ample room to dump the dirt without interfering with the meeting, but he chose to go among the crowd of people, making his way to about six yards from the stage, when the crowd stopped him. Reverend Perry announced to the people not to pay O'Neill any mind. There were a number of men (Irish Catholics) standing nearby with their shirt sleeves rolled up. O'Neill promptly dismounted and undid the cart, which dumped the load of dirt on the lot. One man grabbed the reins of the horse and questioned whether he came there to break up the meeting. O'Neill responded he would "come there any time he damned pleased."

Edward Sheridan and a brother of Mr. McAvoy laughed and applauded as O'Neill dumped the load. Later in court, William Shea stated that he seen O'Neill dump the dirt and that O'Neill was a carter and that the lot was an open lot. O'Neill dumped two other loads there the next morning. O'Neill said he was paid to dump the dirt and that he would attend to his business. He had been in the neighborhood at least ten years. The person responsible for the lot stated he had hired O'Neill to take the dirt to the lot as he was improving it. The nativists would later claim the dirt sat there for months, showing a calculated action by the Irish Catholics to disrupt the nativist meeting.

O'Neill and his cart of dirt was enough to change the proceedings of the meeting. After this, it was difficult for the meeting to get back on track. Besides O'Neill, other Irish Catholics began to disrupt the meeting, among them the same men that disrupted the May 3 meeting: John Daley, John Donnelly, Patrick Lafferty, Thomas McWilliams, James Sherry, Hugh Flanagan and Thomas Walls. John O'Neill would eventually be arrested and charged with participating in the riot. On December 28, 1844, he was fined one dollar and costs and sentenced to nine months in prison.

All of the above Irishmen took their turns in disrupting the meeting. Names and slurs were hurled at the speakers and shouts of "hirelings for the British Whigs" were thrown about. James Sherry would later be charged with the murder of J. Wesley Rhinedollar, and John Daley would be charged with the murder of Mathew Hammitt, both killed during the rioting on May 7 that followed the assaults on the May 3 and May 6 meetings. Daley was also at first accused of shooting George Young and nearly killing him, also on May 7, but later that charge was dropped. Patrick Lafferty, a boss weaver, and Hugh Flanagan are said to have participated in the Gideonite Riot in Philadelphia in 1831 and thus had some prestige among the Irish. Lafferty suffered during the riots, having his home burned to the ground, along with being arrested for rioting.

Moving of the Meeting to the Market House and the Outbreak of Fighting

As the verbal attacks by the Irish Catholics on the speakers continued, a crowd of Irishmen began to gather at the Nanny Goat Market. The next speaker after Colonel Smith was Lewis C. Levin. Levin took the stand but had not proceeded far before a terrible storm of wind and rain deluged the meeting. Many persons ran from the meeting to seek shelter elsewhere, but the majority adjourned over to the Nanny Goat Market on Washington Street, above Master, only ninety yards away. During the time they were running in this direction to avoid the rain, a great deal of name-calling and shouting was kept up by the Irish Catholics, and everyone in the street was excited. When the audience was forced into the tight quarters under the

Illustration of Kensington Riot taken from *Awful Riots* book. The row of armed men is similar to Peter Albright's attempted attack on the Irish Catholics.

shed of the market house, tensions rose. A few minutes after the meeting was reorganized and Levin again attempted to address the crowd, he was pelted by several stones, and then a commotion occurred from some cause or other and some twelve to fifteen men ran out of the west side of the market, pursued by about an equal number. The two groups met, and a fight ensued. It was said that two "desperate fellows clinched each other, one armed with a brick, and the other a club, and exchanged a dozen blows, any one of which seemed severe enough to kill an ordinary man."

Stones and bricks began to be thrown by both sides, and persons on both sides fired several pistol shots. When the guns were heard, members of the audience immediately began to disperse and flee the market house area. Some nativists took up positions at the south end of the market and hoisted the American flag that had previously been raised on the stage at the Second and Master Streets meeting lot. This was the flag that the nativists would later claim George Shiffler died protecting.

The cause of the outburst under the market house was said to have started when two men—David Fields, a nativist, and an Irish Catholic by the name of McLaughlin—got into a heated argument. Fields was heard saying, "For god's sake, be quiet and let him speak," a reference to Lewis C. Levin who had just started up the meeting again. John McCloon, standing nearby, responded, "You old rascal, you're always talking." Fields fired back, "You have no right to speak, you are not a citizen." John Donnelly, who boarded with Patrick Lafferty, known to have been one of the rioters, then yelled back, "You old rascal, knock him down."

Fields, testifying in the riot trials later in the year, stated that he then saw a young man surrounded by several Irishmen, who he named as being Edmond "Ned" Sherry, Hugh McGuigan, John McCloon and Mr. Walls, perhaps Thomas Walls, who was active in the rioting. At this time, the young man, nativist John Finletter, drew a pair of pistols and threatened to shoot the first man who touched Fields, stating, "Let him be." The Irishmen were ready to knock Fields down.

As is normal in these cases, another braver man challenged Finletter and stepped outside the western side of the market house. Sure enough, young Finletter fired off his pistols at his challenger. The challenger was likely Patrick Fisher, as he was the first person known to be shot in the rioting. He was shot in the face. Fisher was a known character in the West Kensington neighborhood. He was a former constable and low-level politico in the area. He initially was also the first person who tried to intervene when Fields and McLaughlin were ready to fight. When the nativists first arrived at the market house, it was also Fisher who addressed them in an authoritarian tone, telling them to "keep on their own ground and not come into the market house," thus he was early marked as a target by the nativists. Trial testimony also reported that a Mr. Croney was the person who threw the first blow, perhaps one of the others who intervened in the Fields and McLaughlin argument. After firing his pistols, Finletter joined in the rioting and was seen later on throwing stones.

A witness by the name of Joseph Sharp, who would later testify at the riot trials, stated that he saw "a gun pointed out of a raised window of the Hibernia Hose House and discharged against the crowd." This was after the Irish and nativists had started to skirmish at the western side of the market house. This shot from the hose house was answered by several shots from pistols from the crowd of nativists. The distance from the hose house to the southern end of the market house was about 122 feet. The firing on the meeting became more general, with the nativists hiding behind the pillars of the market shed. John Daley, one of the men who broke up the May 3 meeting, was seen firing on the meeting from a short distance away by Sophia Clark, who observed ten or twenty people firing shots at the meeting from the vicinity of Master Street, near Cadwalader. This would have been just before the nativists chased the Irish down Master Street toward

Germantown Road. None of these other shooters seem to have actually been at the meeting under the roof of the market house, but they acted in accordance with the other Irish at the meeting at those distant points.

John Donnell gave support to Sharp's testimony, stating that he and Sharp were two of the earliest to enter the market house and that one rather intoxicated fellow (Patrick Fisher) with his shirt sleeves rolled up was heard saying, "Keep the damned Natives out of the market house, this ground don't belong to them—this is ours." As Fisher gave the word, thirty to forty other fellows "all with their shirt sleeves rolled up, started up and got close together, cheering and harassing the Natives as they entered the market house." Donnell, a nativist, stated that Fisher, a presumed leader of the Catholics, struck the first blow, not Croney as was earlier reported.

The Kensington Riots produced an odd outcome from Patrick Fisher. It was reported that later on, when the Kensington Riots were raging at their heights (May 7 and 8), the house of Patrick Fisher was burned and his family, "driven before the raging flames and dreading the vengeance of the mob, made a precipitous flight into the woods. A daughter of Fisher, 12 or 13 years of age, who from her infancy had never been able to either walk or talk, was actually frightened into speech and the power of walking by the terrible scene of battle and conflagration. The girl can now run about like other children of her age, and is in perfect possession of the faculty of speech."

After Fisher was shot, he staggered away with help, and oddly enough, he met up with Peter Albright, an apparent friend or acquaintance, who was coming out of Carroll's tavern on Second Street (below Master). Albright had been at the tavern with William Cheetam Hall, an artist from Spring Garden. The two were out to see Sheriff Fitler on business, and they "happened" to come by the meeting near the schoolhouse, when the shower came and instead of going to the market house where the meeting was to reconvene, they instead went to Carroll's tavern. Albright came out of the tavern into the alleyway, where he looked over to the direction of Cadwalader Street and saw three Irish women picking up rocks with their aprons. He heard a report of firearms, and as the people in the tavern rushed out, he went around to the schoolhouse and saw some people bringing Patrick Fisher, who was bleeding, over from the market. He assisted carrying Fisher to an apothecary shop. Albright and Fisher would have known each other; they were both political leaders and former constables from their respective neighborhoods (Fisher in West Kensington, Albright in the Northern Liberties). Albright also would later help carry the body of the slain George Shiffler, getting his hands covered in blood in the process. The following day, he became an active leader in the riots on the side of the nativists, using his military background to create formations of men to carry out attacks on the Irish Catholics. He was wounded by gunshot in the process.

While the two groups first started to battle near the open lot in front of the Hibernia Hose Company, several stones were thrown at the hose house, the first building behind the corner property on Master Street and west of the market. Today's Crane Building did not then exist, and the view from the market house in the middle of Washington (American) Street to the hose house was unobstructed, the triangular lot of the Crane Building being an empty lot for about the southern two thirds of the block. This stoning stirred up the Irish, who were holed up in the hose house and ready for some action. Firing took place from the upper windows of the building, causing a reaction from the nativist mob, which threw more stones at the hose house and fired its guns as well. A courtyard, just north of the hose house, also contained some armed Irishmen, who began firing at this time.

A nativist crowd chased some Catholics west on Master Street, and another group chased Catholics south on Cadwalader Street, below Master Street. These Irish had been firing and throwing stones at the nativists in the market house. The nativists attacked a frame house on Master Street, between Cadwalader and Germantown Road. The house was stormed and the windows and doors demolished. Two other frame houses on Cadwalader Street, below Master, shared the same fate. One of these belonged to Edward Develin, whose only involvement in the riot was that a man fell into his doorway (the entryway was below the level of the pavement) and rolled into his house. Develin quickly closed the door upon the arrival of the nativists who then proceeded to smash his windows and door with brickbats and stones, some weighing as much as seven or eight pounds each. Develin, his wife and children were "wrenched off by a man," narrowly escaping injury.

At this point, two or three muskets were fired by the Irish Catholics in their retreat down Master Street as they attempted to fight back. The men who had raised the American flag at the south end of the Market House still held their ground even though volleys of bricks and stones were continually being thrown upon them, along with an occasional shot from the hose house. After being chased over Master Street to Germantown, a number of Irish Catholics rallied at Germantown and Master and came down Master Street toward the nativists at a brisk pace with stones and several guns. The nativists retreated but maintained a fire with stones and pistols themselves. Several nativists were killed and wounded at this point, and their comrades became furious. The nativists again rallied and recovered a temporary advantage, as well as the opportunity to retrieve their wounded, but finally retreated "under sharp fire of every kind of missiles, and two or three discharges of a musket carried by a gray-headed Irishman who wore a seal-skin cap."

According to contemporary newspaper accounts, Irish women also joined in the rioting:

> *The Irish population were in a dreadful state of excitement, and even women and boys joined in the affray, some of the women actually throwing missiles. Many of them when they temporarily retreated, returned armed with firearms, which they discharged sometimes with particular aim at individuals engaged on the other side, and at other times firing indiscriminately in the several groups, on the larger body of the belligerents.*
>
> *Many of the women who were not engaged with weapons incited the men to vigorous action, pointing out where they could operate with more effect, and cheering them on and rallying them to a renewal of the conflict whenever their spirits fell or they were compelled to retreat.*

During their advance over Master Street, the nativists stormed the home of John Lafferty at Germantown and Master, as well as that of his next-door neighbor, an old widow named Mrs. Brady. The two shared a common alley. Lafferty was not at home, but Mrs. Brady was. The houses were battered with brickbats and stones, the panels of the front doors knocked out and the windows broken. They destroyed the "looking-glasses and tables" and, piece-by-piece, destroyed all the furniture. Lafferty's house sat on the corner of Germantown Road but was able to be accessed through the back alley off of Master. A man that the nativists were chasing ran over Master Street and into Lafferty's alley, jumping his fence to hide. His discovery caused the attack on Lafferty's and Brady's houses.

Michael Quin's house was one of the other houses on the north side of Master Street that was attacked, battered and had some of the furniture destroyed. His wife was sitting in the house at the time, but they escaped injury. John Lavary's house, next door to Quin's, suffered the same fate. Apparently someone had used the doorways of Lavary's and Quin's houses to conceal themselves when firing a gun at the nativists. This was good enough for the nativists to destroy the houses. Lavary would later be arrested for participating in the riots. He was described as a "boss weaver," and his house was described as a large handsome brick building, with brick back buildings. These houses would all later be destroyed further from the firing of the buildings on Cadwalader Street, with those fires spreading during the second and third days of the riots. Mrs. Lavary was said to "bewail" the breaking of the windows of the house by the rioters on Monday afternoon (May 6), little dreaming at that time that these outrages would be followed by the total destruction of the property in days to come. Another neighbor on the same block by the name of John Brown had his door shot up by the rioters. All while this was going on, a number of nativists continued throwing stones and firing guns at the hose house on Cadwalader Street, whose upper windows were completely shattered and the doors and building itself riddled by gunshots.

The "rally" mentioned above by the Irish Catholics at Germantown Road and Master Streets appears to have been a coordinated planned attack on the nativists. After the initial conflict at the market house, some Irish ran out the west side of the market house, where they engaged the nativists briefly. Heavy fire from the Hibernia Hose Company, the courtyard north of it and other nearby houses chased the nativists southward and kept them penned in at the southern end of the market house. When the Irish retreated west on Master Street, a group of nativists gave chase after them. With the Irish running west on Master Street and pursued by the nativists, the nativists were drawn into a trap. While some nativists stopped to assault the houses on Master Street, others continued westward on Master Street chasing the Irishmen. However, when they got to Germantown Road, another group of armed Irishmen, consisting of John Daley, David Funk, Francis Small, Terrence Mullin and others, were waiting for them around the corner on Germantown, north of Master. This group of Irish let go several volleys of gunfire with the result that a number of nativists were hit, one was killed (George Shiffler), one would died later on (Joseph Cox) and a number were wounded.

The first afternoon of rioting took about an hour to play out. Both sides then retreated and waited for darkness to come. That first hour of the Kensington Riots saw one nativist shot and killed (George Shiffler), one shot in the hip who died later on May 22 (Joseph Cox) and eleven other nativists shot or injured by brickbats and stones, but there were likely more that didn't make the newspaper or court records. Henry Temper was shot in the side, the shot glancing off his hip, producing a flesh wound. Thomas Ford had a spent ball glance off his forehead, which did not do him much damage, but then after glancing off his head, it lodged in the head of another man, who was seriously injured. A man by the name of C. Jackson was wounded by gunshot, as was John Deal. George McAllister was wounded by a gunshot

Looking north on Germantown, at Master Street. George Shiffler was killed at this location by a group of Irish Catholics shooting south on Germantown.

that passed through his cheek and lodged in his mouth, disfiguring him for life and making him disabled so that he could no longer work. Samuel Beatty was shot in the lip, the ball going through his face and into his mouth. Charles Vanstavern was shot in the body with buckshot. Edward Spain was shot in the hip, and a man named Duncan was injured in the back by a brickbat. Fields, the man who started the early encounter in the market house with McLaughlin, was badly wounded, and an old man was hit in the head with a brickbat, knocking him senseless.

This first afternoon also saw five Irish Catholic houses battered and ransacked and one house having its door riddled with gunshot. All the properties that were damaged were in the area of Master Street, Cadwalader Streets and Germantown Avenue. Other homes in the immediate area were also slightly damaged, including the Hibernia Hose Company, the windows of which were shattered and the doors and building shot up.

It is not clear who on the Irish Catholic side was wounded at this time, except for Patrick Fisher. The newspapers of the day tended not to report the Catholic casualties, and the Irish, likely still being an insular immigrant community, did not volunteer any information. Civil authorities were nonexistent at this stage of the riot, and thus no statistics were being kept. There was no mention of Catholics being killed at this first outburst on Monday afternoon.

With the nativists in retreat, the initial violent confrontations of the Kensington Riots came to an end that afternoon. Much like the first, round two also went to the Catholics. However, the rioting would start back up again in the evening as darkness fell over the area. George Shiffler, a nineteen-year-old nativist, died of his wounds at the intersection of Master Street and Germantown Road, the first to die in the Kensington Riots of '44. After his death, he was elevated to "martyr" status, a new symbol to rally around for the growing political nativist movement.

George Shiffler: Nativist Martyr

George Shiffler was the first nativist to die in the Kensington Riots and the first to die for the nativist cause in America, thus he was made a martyr by the Native American movement. It was stated that he was the eldest son of a widow, which helped to dramatize the tragedy. However, it was never mentioned just how she became a widow. Shiffler was shot at the intersection of Germantown Road and Master Street, with several buckshot lodging in his right side, one entering under his right arm and the charge of the piece fired entering his chest, piercing his heart. The entire load, consisting of about a dozen slugs and a handful of shot, entered Shiffler's breast, killing him instantly.

It has been romanticized that Shiffler was clutching the American flag, keeping it from touching the ground and defending it from a supposed Irish Catholic mob intent on destroying it. This symbolism helped him to become a martyr and a hero of the Native American cause, a political movement that was anti-immigrant in nature and anti-Catholic by design.

George Shiffler appears to have been the son of George Shiffler and Rebecca Vaughan. The elder George Shiffler was a tobacconist, and the family lived on Saunder's Court, off St. John's (American) Street, a few doors below Beaver (Wildey) Street.

An article in the *Public Ledger* of December 12, 1842, states that the elder George Shiffler committed suicide: "A man named George Shiffler, a tobacconist, about 40 years of age, committed suicide yesterday afternoon in

Illustration of Shiffler being shot; however, he was shot on the street, not the stage. The building with the hanging bucket is presumed to be Hibernia Hose Company.

St. John's Street, a few doors below Beaver Street, by cutting his throat. He has left a wife and three or four children."

A death notice for the elder George Shiffler was published in the *Public Ledger* the following day. It stated that the elder George Shiffler was forty-four years old. His funeral was held at his home on St. John's Street, below Beaver, and he was buried at the Kensington Methodist Cemetery. This church's cemetery was one of the three cemeteries that made up the old Hanover Burial Ground, today's Hetzel's Playground at Columbia Avenue and Thompson Street.

An article in the *North American* of December 13, 1842, states that "Alderman Brazer on Sunday (December 11, 1842) held an inquest in St. John Street, below Beaver, on the body of George Shiffler, 45 years of age, who committed suicide by cutting the jugular vein with a small penknife. The deceased was a tobacconist, and has left a wife and seven children. Verdict, suicide, while laboring under mental derangement."

Rebecca Vaughan, wife of George Shiffler Sr. and mother of the younger George Shiffler who was the first to be killed in the riots, was the daughter of Thomas Vaughan (1757–1842) and Mary Bryan (d. 1843). During the Revolutionary War, Thomas Vaughan served in the Philadelphia Militia under Captain John Hewson, a local Kensington Revolutionary War hero and the person to whom Fishtown's Hewson Street is named for. Both Thomas Vaughan and John Hewson are buried in Palmer Cemetery. The Vaughan family was a fairly famous Kensington shipbuilding family, running shipyards and wharf-building enterprises throughout most of the nineteenth century on the Kensington waterfront.

Young George Shiffler was said to be an apprentice leather worker for Christopher "Shordy" Shorda, a morocco dresser, residing on Saunder's Court, running east of St. John (American) Street, above Beaver (Wildey). A later newspaper account from an interview with a member of the Shiffler family who was alive at the time of the riot stated that Shiffler was standing wide-mouth outside Shordy's shop when he heard the news of the nativists' meeting being broken up on May 6. He went home, ate dinner and told his mother he was going up to Kensington because the "Irish are going to murder the Natives up in Kensington." His mother was horrified, but Shiffler was determined. It was no use for her to try and stop him as he told her, "I'm a Native American myself mother and if they need my help, they'll not have to ask it twice from me." He left immediately, not taking his coat, wearing only linen trousers and shirtsleeves.

After young George Shiffler was shot at the opening moments of the riots, his body was carried to George C. Bower's Drugstore, at the corner of Germantown Road and Phoenix (Thompson) Street where Dr. McAvoy dressed the wounds, but with no help, Shiffler died a few moments later.

Many relatives and friends attended his funeral on May 9, and there was a large crowd of Native Americans who followed his remains to the old Hanover Burial Ground, where he was laid to rest at the family plot. Young Shiffler's coffin had a silver plate with the inscription: "George Shiffler, aged 19 Years, The first Martyr in the Native American Cause. Killed May 6th, 1844." The coffin was wrapped in the same American flag under "whose folds and in supporting which he lost his life." A second notice of Shiffler's funeral, perhaps paid for by the Nativist Party organizations, was listed in the *North American and Daily Advertiser* on May 8, 1844. It read as follows:

Native Americans

The Native Americans of the city and county of Philadelphia, are invited to attend the funeral of GEORGE SHIFFLER, from his late residence in Saunders' court, St. John's above Beaver street, on Thursday morning, May 9th, at half past eight o'clock A.M. Those Natives residing in the City Southwark and Moyamensing, will meet at Independence Hall at eight o'clock, and move from thence in a body. They will be met by the Spring Garden, Northern Liberties and Kensington delegations, on their route.

It is said by some commentators, contemporary to the time, that Shiffler was very active in the nativist cause on the day that he was killed. John Hancock Lee, a nativist writing in 1855, states that:

One young man, about nineteen years of age, was engaged throughout the afternoon, in supporting the American flag, which hung over the speakers' stand. This rendered him an especial mark for the aim of the enemies of the cause he was maintaining. Two or three times had the flag fallen to the ground, and as often did George Shiffler, with the assistance of several others, again raise it, and cause its stripes and stars to float above their heads. But his efforts were unavailing; for a bullet at length pierced his heart, and he fell as senseless as the flag he supported, to the ground. He was carried to the store of an apothecary near by, where in a few minutes he ceased to exist, and before the sun had gone down the lifeless body of the boy was laid at the feet of a widowed and distracted mother, who had centered her hopes of comfort in old age upon him, and who had left her but a few hours before, in the buoyancy and strength of healthful youth and happy expectancy. The flag which he had supported was torn and leveled with the dust, by those who had sworn to protect our country and her laws. And he and others were murdered by men who were pretending to love and revere and contend for the religion of Him, all whose teachings aim for the promotion of peace and good will toward men.

If Shiffler was active is supporting or carrying the American flag that day, he must have taken it from the south end of the market house where it had been placed when the meeting reorganized there and carried it with him when he chased the Irish over Master Street, getting shot at the intersection of Germantown and Master.

After her son George's death, Rebecca Vaughan Shiffler took her two younger children and moved to Southwark. Her eldest daughter stayed in Kensington living with her uncle, the ship carpenter Matthias Creamer (circa 1788–1860), who had married Margaret Vaughan, Rebecca's sister.

Contemporary print of the shooting of George Shiffler, the soon-to-be nativist martyr. *Courtesy of Daniel Dailey.*

The family history states that Rebecca Vaughan and George Shiffler had about ten children, and indeed a George Shiffler was found in the 1840 census living in Kensington's Second Ward (where the intersection of St. John's and Beaver is located) with possibly nine children in the house. However, besides the martyred George Shiffler, there is only evidence for three of Rebecca's supposed ten children.

George Shiffler, the martyr, was honored in Southwark when a volunteer fire company took his name for its company. American Republicans from the border areas of the Fifth and Sixth Wards founded the Shiffler Hose Company. The scene of his death was often painted on broadsides, flags and other ephemeral items, and he became a martyr and hero to the Native American cause.

Francis Small is said to have been the person who shot and killed young George Shiffler, but he escaped to Ireland. John Taggert and Peter Devlin were arrested for the murder of Shiffler. Taggert was caught by a mob and almost beaten to death. While indicted for the murder of George Shiffler, evidence was scarce, and the beating he took was said to be sufficient for his involvement in the riot, thus he served no further jail time but for what he had already served waiting for trial.

The dirty and torn American flag that Shiffler is supposed to have saved from the angry Irish Catholic mob was said by the Irish to have been dirty and torn because of the nativists dragging the flag through the streets during a cloudburst at the time when the nativists ran to the Nanny Goat Market to get out of the oncoming rain storm. Over 168 years later, it is hard to say who is correct, but certainly Shiffler appears to have been just another one of the rioters and not a martyr.

A FULL

AND

COMPLETE ACCOUNT

OF THE LATE

AWFUL RIOTS

IN PHILADELPHIA.

EMBELLISHED WITH TEN ENGRAVINGS.

PHILADELPHIA:
JOHN B. PERRY, No. 198 MARKET STREET.
HENRY JORDAN, Third and Dock Street.
NEW YORK:—NAFIS & CORNISH.

Title page of *Awful Riots* book, a nativist account of the Kensington Riots, published by nativist printer John B. Perry soon after the event took place.

Attempted Attack on the Nunnery on Monday Evening

The Native Americans rallied again in the early evening of May 6 at the Assembly Building at the corner of Tenth and Chestnut Streets. The meeting was organized by the appointment of B.W. Green, chairman, and John Brodhead, secretary. The speakers at this meeting were E.M. Spencer, Dr. John H. Gihon,

Colonel Peter Sken Smith, Colonel C.G. Childs, E.D. Tarr, T.R. Newbold and William Deal Baker. Resolutions were adopted that the Native American Party would attend en masse the bodies of those martyrs of republicanism who were slain on Monday, May 6, in Kensington; that a committee be appointed to make arrangements with the families of the deceased for their internments; and that a further committee of three be appointed to inquire into the circumstances of the families of the deceased. Lastly, a $1,000 reward would offered by the American Republican Party for the murderers of George Shiffler.

While there is no record from this meeting that stated that the meeting should reconvene in Kensington, a crowd did begin to gather to gawk at the scenes of the earlier rioting. Between 7:00 p.m. until after 8:00 p.m., there was a deadly silence that filled the Kensington neighborhood. A number of Irishmen were observed gathering at the market house, armed, waiting for the nativists' return. Just after 8:00 p.m., a large crowd began to gather at the corner of Franklin (Girard Avenue) and Second Streets. The crowd soon extended for about a half mile down Second Street, with people still joining the mob. At about this time, a large bonfire was set by mostly half-grown boys, which was kept burning during the night and lit up the whole neighborhood. The mob, now excited by the fire, proceeded to move north on Second Street, but when they were about halfway between Franklin and Phoenix (Thompson) Streets, a shower of brickbats and paving stones was poured down on them from the roofs and windows of several houses.

This attack momentarily caused a fearful rush down the street, but a number of persons soon rallied themselves and attacked several houses from which the missiles had been thrown. In a short time, the windows and doors were destroyed, and those inside escaped out the backdoors.

The mob moved north on Second Street, attacking the homes of suspected Irish Catholics on both sides of the street. Nativist sympathizers and non-Catholics hung American flags in their windows to keep the mob from destroying their houses. The crowd broke the windows and knocked down the doors of the Irish Catholics and went into the houses, destroying the furniture. The inhabitants of the homes fled from the ruthlessness of the mob.

A cry of "Go to the nunnery!" went up, and the mob proceeded to Second and Phoenix (Thompson) Streets to set fire to the nunnery, the former convent of the Sisters of Charity of the Blessed Virgin Mary, which sat at the southeast corner of that intersection. This convent was founded with the help of Father Donaghoe, pastor at St. Michael's Church. In 1843, the Sisters had removed, under the direction of Father Donaghoe, to the diocese of Dubuque, Iowa, where the Mother House and Novitiate eventually flourished. One postulant,

Sister Mary Baker, had been left in Philadelphia to help settle the affairs of the order and care for the convent property. Father Donaghoe was actually not the pastor of St. Michael's at this time, having already moved to Iowa, but by chance he happened to be back in Philadelphia on a visit, helping to wind up the business of the Sisters of Charity.

Sister Baker was "a little English lady" and had for help two young girl companions, Elizabeth Sullivan and Jane O'Reilly. The women met the mob at the door of the convent, with the belief that "no man would be brutal enough to burn to death three helpless women." However, as soon as she opened the door, a brick thrown with "deliberate aim" struck Sister Baker in the head, knocking her back into the house unconscious. With the efforts of several brave Irishmen, the three were rescued, making their way through the garden and fleeing to a place of safety, secured by Father Donaghoe. The three women would later move to Iowa and join the order of nuns.

The high board fence around the convent was lit on fire, and "burning brands" were attempted to be thrown through the windows, but the mob was stopped when from the rooftops a "volley of ball and buckshot" rained down on the rioters. Several other volleys of shot followed, and the crowd was sent scattering. A number of people were shot, some falling to the street seriously wounded.

Some shots were fired from the rooftop of Joseph Corr's Temperance Grocery Store, which sat across from the convent at the northeast corner of Second and Phoenix Streets. Corr's store would in the following days be riddled with gunshots and completely destroyed by the mob. The fact that the shots came from Corr's building was enough for the crowd to devastate the property. Rumors also spread that Corr supplied the Irish Catholics with the ball and shot.

A young man by the name of Nathan D. Ramsay, a twenty-one-year-old blindmaker from the Northern Liberties (Third Street, above Brown), was shot through the breastbone, perforating his lungs. He was carried to an apothecary store on Second Street above Germantown. He lingered for a number of days, dying on May 28.

Another young man, William Wright, the nineteen-year-old son of Northern Liberties salt merchant Archibald Wright, was shot through his head and killed almost instantly. He was said not to be participating in the riot, but rather a gawker, talking with a friend about sixty yards south of the nunnery when it was being attacked by the nativists. He was carried to the same apothecary as Nathan Ramsey, as were three others who were wounded that day. Wright is said to have lived on Fourth Street, near Tammany (Buttonwood).

Looking northwest from the site of the nunnery. In the distance, St. Michael's is on the right, and the intersection of Cadwalader and Master Streets is across the lot on the left.

Upward of twelve other people were shot and wounded, with some falling at the rear of the nunnery, but since it was too dangerous to retrieve them, they were left lying where they fell. A newspaper reporter later wrote of seeing several holes in the wooden fence made by musket balls, and the following day, "marks of blood were visible" on the pavement.

While most accounts in the newspapers stated that the volleys of gunshot came from the roof of Corr's grocery store, later trial testimony shows there were two groups of Irishmen firing at those who attempted to destroy the nunnery. The nativists would later accuse the Catholics of having armed men in the church, on the church grounds and even in the nunnery, thus justifying their attack on the nunnery that night. However, witnesses later testified that at the time the nunnery was attacked, when the Irish defended it and killed Wright and Ramsay, there were no men in St. Michael's Church or on the church grounds nor in the nunnery, except for a couple carpenters in the church. A witness stated two parties were engaged for the Irish that night, and the two people were killed on the second volley of shots, one from the corner house (Corr's store) and one from the seminary, although evidence showed this was not true.

Thomas Jackson kept a grocery store at the corner of Perry (Palethorp) and Phoenix (Thompson) Streets and saw no firing from the seminary, but he did see firing later from Perry Street after other firing started from neighboring streets.

Sophia Drury lived in the nunnery from September 1843 to May 1844, with her sister Ms. Baker, who was placed in charge of it by Mr. Snyder, the Reverend Donaghoe's counsel. Drury heard firing from a house at the corner of Perry Street, belonging to Mr. Corr, which was undergoing repairs. She heard no firing from the seminary. Mrs. Baker and the others tried to leave, but the crowd would not let the carriage near the house. Like the nunnery, Corr's grocery store likely stretched from Second Street eastward to Perry Street.

John Donnegan lived at the rear of the nunnery and saw the shooting. He saw Wright and Ramsay killed and stated that all the shooting came from Second Street and Perry Street, all on ground level. Because this part of the neighborhood was not lit, he saw the flashes. The back of the schoolhouse (the nunnery, which was also used as a seminary) was on Perry Street (the nunnery faced Second Street, running eastward to Perry Street).

Thomas P. Rakestraw was on the ground after 9:00 p.m., before the firing, until 12:00 a.m., and he saw no firing from the nunnery, stating that the firing was partly from Second Street, above Phoenix, and partly from a vacant lot on the west side of Second Street. He saw Wright and Ramsay fall; Ramsay was shot about ten minutes after Wright. Rakestraw was a Quaker.

General George Cadwalader and Sheriff Morton McMichael were on the ground as well, on Second Street, below Phoenix, and they saw no firing from the nunnery. Cadwalader was in front of the nunnery, a little below where Wright was killed in Second Street. While General Cadwalader and the sheriff might have been on the ground, they were only surveying the situation. The sheriff and Cadwalader, a general in the militia who would later lead the troops to suppress the riot, did not try to stop any of the outrages. However, what they saw on Monday night was reason enough for them to call out the militia the following day. Sheriff McMichael was on the ground during the evening and shortly before nightfall made a call to the military for aid, which prompted Cadwalader's appearance. However, the militia had some time before resolved not to perform duty in cases of riots unless the legislature made an appropriation for their pay during the time they were so engaged, which had not yet been done, so they were not willing to enter duty. After Monday night's events, a meeting was called to take measures to ensure a full turnout of the military force. The sheriff, accompanied by General Cadwalader,

General George Cadwalader (1806–1879) led the militia in suppressing the Nativist Riots. Oddly enough, much of the rioting took place on Cadwalader Street, named for his family.

restrained the mob several times on Monday night.

George Cadwalader (1806–1879) was a soldier, lawyer and businessman. He was born into an old and distinguished military family from Philadelphia. A graduate of the University of Pennsylvania, he studied law and was a member of the bar. He joined the First Troop Philadelphia City Cavalry in 1826, became a captain of the Philadelphia Grays in 1832 and was later commissioned brigadier general of the First Brigade, First Division, Pennsylvania Militia, in 1842. It was in this capacity that Cadwalader commanded the forces that put down the Nativist Riot in Kensington.

Mary McFarland, testifying at the riot trials later in the year, stated she saw men coming in and out of the parsonage house (rectory) and was "not sure if they had their guns hidden or not." She was heading down Second Street when the firing started at the nunnery. She heard one of the men say, "Come on boys." Although McFarland lived three blocks from the parsonage house, she was sitting on Mr. Sharkey's steps, across the street from the rectory, and it was near 10:00 p.m. McFarland had just come back from the bonfire at Second and Franklin (Girard) Streets.

Bonfires were lit throughout the area by the mobs that first night, but no one was arrested for those actions. The *Philadelphia Inquirer* reported that "several Native American meetings were held" in "different wards of Southwark," and "strong resolutions were adopted in relation to the outrages in Kensington."

For a second time, the nativists were routed by the gunfire of the Irish Catholics. Round three also went to the Irish Catholics. The nativists suffered two killed and a number wounded. The Catholic casualty count was again unknown. Because the neighborhood was their home, the Catholics were able to hide in houses, buildings and alleyways, while the nativists were forced to fight without cover. However, this advantage would soon change once the nativists began to burn down the neighborhood on the second day of the rioting.

On Monday night, a rumor spread that the nativist mob intended to fire St. Michael's Church. Many armed Irish Catholic men retreated to the church and prepared to defend it.

Later in the night, crowds of armed men on both sides roamed the neighborhood's streets, with occasional gunshots ringing out from homes, alleys and from behind fences. A group of Irish shot at a group of men standing at Second and Franklin (Girard), wounding a butcher at Wharton Market named Taylor in the eye, as well as seriously wounding several other people. They shot out from Perry (Palethorp) Street in the cover of the dark. By midnight, the crowds started to disperse, and the day's activities seem to have ended. However, many were still afraid to walk home, thinking they could be shot down at any moment. By 1:30 a.m., things had quieted down, and the first full day of the Kensington Riots had come to an end.

One man, John McAleer, a weaver, was arrested rather quickly. McAleer was one of the Irishmen on the rooftop of Corr's grocery who fired into the nativist crowd. His musket burst, it was assumed, the first time he discharged it, blowing off his left thumb and lacerating the surrounding muscles and tendons. He needed to go to the hospital and while there was arrested by Alderman Redman. He tried to lie, stating that he had hurt himself the previous day (May 5) by misfiring his gun. However, the authorities had been alerted by Josiah Johnson, who found the thumb in the yard of his house on Perry Street between Phoenix and Master, and were on the lookout for him. The mob would later take revenge on McAleer, destroying his two large brick houses at the corner of Second and Master Streets, by burning them to the ground.

Another man by the name of John Daley was also arrested. Daley had injured himself when his musket misfired. His trail of blood was traced to his friend's nearby home. Most of Daley's native-born neighbors were afraid to enter, but an American Republican housepainter named Albert Alberger, later appointed a Kensington watchman, burst in and made a citizen's arrest of Daley and his companion near Second and Master Streets. Daley appears to have lived in a house behind John McAleer's property. His house was fired during the riots and destroyed as well. This man would appear to be a different John Daley than the one who was more active in the rioting on Harmony Court on May 7.

CHAPTER 6

TUESDAY, MAY 7, 1844

THE SECOND DAY OF RIOTING

On Tuesday morning, May 7, 1844, the local nativist newspapers *Native American* and *Sun* ran extras. Mobs of people lined up to purchase the latest news of the riots. The papers called for Native Americans to assemble in a mass meeting at 3:30 p.m. at the State House Yard (behind Independence Hall). Crowds began to gather, and by the appointed time, it was said there were upward of six thousand people assembled. The following officers were elected: President T.R. Newbold; Vice-president A. De Kalb Tarr; R.W. Green; Reverend John H. Gihon; John D. Fox; Thomas Taylor; Thomas D. Grover; John S. Warner; and Secretaries James L. Gihon, A.R. Peale and Lewis C. Levin. The meeting was organized and was briefly addressed by Newbold, followed by Jas. C. Vandyke, Esq., who spoke slightly longer. Other speakers included William Hollingshead, John H. Gihon, John Perry and Colonel Charles J. Jack.

The Reverend John H. Gihon insisted that the words "Let Every Man Come Prepared to Defend Himself" be added to the posters that were made up to advertise the nativist meeting in Kensington. It was a direct call to arms. Gihon was the pastor of the Third Universalist Church, located at Phoenix (Thompson) above Frankford Road. Colonel Charles J. Jack, an attorney, unleashed an emotionally charged tirade that whipped the crowd into a frenzy, and they began to chant, "Let's go to Kensington." In all, about a half hour was taken up by the speeches, which were followed by a number of resolutions being passed.

The speeches consisted of the usual rants against immigrants and fears of their participations in elections. The violence of the Irish Catholics on the previous day was loudly denounced. Several of the speakers requested calm and nonviolence. However, at the end of the meeting, there was a call to adjourn until Thursday, but the cry went out, "Adjourn to Second and Master Streets now," followed by, "Let us go up into Kensington." When the chairman of the meeting tried to adjourn until Thursday, there was a "thunderous applause" of "noes," but when a motion from the crowd was

made to adjourn to Kensington, the crowd shouted enthusiastically with "yeas." The audience, turning into a raging mob of several thousand, a number of them armed, proceeded to march in procession to Kensington, and the second day of the Kensington Riots was about to begin.

As the nativists were meeting downtown, the Irish were busy preparing for another fight. Many of the residents of the Nanny Goat Market neighborhood began packing their belongings and leaving their homes. A wagon containing a shipment of rifles was delivered to the house of John Paul, an Irish weaver, who lived on "Weaver's Row" and boarded fellow Irish weavers. Weaver's Row was a courtyard that led westward from Cadwalader Street, between Jefferson and Oxford Streets, near Oxford. Paul distributed the rifles to his boarders and others.

Silk bookmark showing a monument to the nativist "martyr" George Shiffler, printed by the *American Advocate*, a contemporary nativist newspaper. *Courtesy Daniel Dailey.*

The Irish on this day would make Harmony Court their headquarters. Harmony was another courtyard on the same block as Weaver's Row, located about one or two properties north of Jefferson, also running westward from Cadwalader. There were sixteen houses on Harmony Court, all families. This was also the home of John Daley. The two courtyards were about three hundred feet apart. Besides those stationed at Harmony Court and Weaver's Row, there was another group of men who later positioned themselves at Germantown and Jefferson Streets. Some of these were the same men who were holed up at Harmony Court, as Harmony Court ran all the way through from Cadwalader Street to Germantown Road. The Irish had upward of thirty armed men prepared to do battle at these locations.

Two other courtyards on this block of Cadwalader were also active in the riot; McAfee's Court sat above Harmony, then Van Buren Court sat above McAfee, and farther north was the above mentioned Weaver's Row, a small courtyard of homes rented out by Irish weavers. Van Buren Court was about thirty feet north of McAfee Court.

Patrick Murray's general store, located at the southeast corner of Germantown and Jefferson, acted as a place for the men to gather and get their ammunition. Here guns were loaded, and from this building many shots were fired. Most of the shots fired down Jefferson Street came from around the corner of this store. Murray would pay dearly for his participation: when the nativists began to fire the neighborhood, they destroyed his store and home. He was also arrested for giving the Irish ammunition.

There were also armed Irishmen stationed farther south on Cadwalader Street, between Master and Jefferson; at the Hibernia Hose Company; at other courtyards; and at several houses along this stretch of Cadwalader, as well as some below Master Street on the west side of Cadwalader. Two men were initially stationed in the market house as well, but they soon moved from there as the mob approached.

There were a number of witnesses from the neighborhood who would later testify at the riot trials as to these positions and the actions of the Irish Catholics as they prepared to fight off the advance and attacks of the nativists. One eyewitness, Mrs. Morton, stated that upon the nativists advancing on Second Street toward the market house, she overheard several Irishmen congregating at Cadwalader Street say, "Now the women and children in the houses, and every man to his gun." About the same time, Stephen Winslow, another eyewitness saw a crowd standing at the corner of Cadwalader and Master. As the meeting advanced, they ran up to Germantown road to an alley, exclaiming, "Get the guns!" Of these, six or eight went into the alley, and each came out with a musket. It would appear that the entire population of the whole two and a half blocks of the west side of Cadwalader Street was armed, from just below Master Street north to Oxford.

The March on Kensington

When the mob arrived at Kensington, it was about 5:00 p.m. William Buck testified later at trials that he met the crowd in Second Street and begged them not to go up to that market as many would be killed and the balance would have to run away. The reply was that the Irish would be afraid to do anything as the nativists had such a crowd. They would be wrong, particularly since the majority of the mob did not enter into the area at Master and Washington. As the mob proceeded toward Kensington in a very large body, they carried an American flag with a placard affixed to it, across which was written, "This is the flag that was trampled upon by Irish Papists." Supposedly, the flag was the same one that George Shiffler had been holding when he was shot down.

One eyewitness to the riot, George H. Martin, testified to the following story at the trials later in the year:

> *I went up on horseback before the meeting went to Kensington. I was there fifteen or twenty minutes before the meeting came. I first saw the crowd coming up 2nd Street, above Franklin and I retired in front of them as they went north and the body of them went to where the market stood. I stood at the north end of the market, on the north side, and had been there but a few minutes when the head of the column of the meeting entered the south end of the market. The only persons I saw in the street, between me and the crowd, were two Irishmen and two women. The crowd immediately commenced stoning the women, when I advanced waving my hat, and asked them if they were men or Americans who would attack women. At the same time I told the two Irishmen to retire to their houses, which they did; the women also passed on without being hurt. The mob then began to throw stones at the houses on the west side of the market, and I saw one man run and jump with both feet against the door of one of the houses. I thought the houses would be defended, and I moved off and before I had gone twenty yards, I heard the report of fire-arms. The crowd soon dispersed and I then saw a body of men form in files two abreast, with shot-guns and rifles.*

They came up through the market. They came out and formed in open order on the open lot and fired at the houses on the west of the market.

This testimony of George H. Martin would seem to agree with the newspaper reports stating that most of the people remained at some distance, down on Franklin (Girard) Street or away from the action at Master and Cadwalader. A group of about seventy-five armed men advanced to the market house and almost immediately began attacking the Hibernia Hose Company. The person Martin described who used two feet to jump against a door was trying to kick in the main carriage door of the hose house, but he was not successful, the firemen having barricaded the door. The mob was, however, able bust open a smaller door, go in, undo the barricade and drag the carriage out of the house and over to Second Street, where they tore it apart. One of the men who participated in this action was Mathew Hammitt. He would later be shot dead.

As soon as the nativists dragged the carriage out from the hose house, gunfire began to rain down on them from the Irish who were positioned along Cadwalader above Jefferson, particularly from John Paul's men at Weaver's Row. Paul is the Irishman who, on the morning of May 7, had a crate of rifles delivered to his home, distributing them to his fellow weavers who boarded with him.

While the Catholics stated the nativists never tried to organize their meeting on May 7, the nativist newspaper reported that they did try to organize the meeting when they arrived in Kensington. However, when they reached the market house, they tried to raise a flag, and gunfire immediately rained down on them from the houses on Cadwalader Street. This account left out the fact that many eyewitnesses stated the nativists arrived and immediately attacked the hose house, smashing down its door and pulling out the carriage. These eyewitnesses also testified that the first shots rang out from several of the houses opposite the market on Cadwalader Street.

COLONEL PETER ALBRIGHT: NATIVIST LEADER

The armed "body of men" seen by George H. Martin that formed in files "two abreast" and walked up through the market was a group of nativists organized by Peter Albright. Albright was previously a colonel in the militia. With his military training, he tried to organize the nativists to fight the

Irish holed up in Harmony Court and Weaver's Row. They were not very successful, as several were shot and wounded or killed. Albright is the same man who, on May 6, helped to carry Patrick Fisher and George Shiffler after those men were shot.

Albright is an interesting character in history. He was a low-level local politician from the Northern Liberties and a one-time constable for the area, as well as a colonel in the militia and a tavern keeper. He was arrested a number of times for fighting and assaulting Irishmen or the police who tried to arrest him, and he was once charged with tampering with elections. He was a commander of the Eighty-fourth Regiment, Pennsylvania Militia, and at one time, he was put up on charges of conduct unbecoming to an officer while on parade. He allowed his men to wear the wrong uniforms and carry the wrong flags and would not let the brigade be inspected. He was also charged with neglect of duty and disobedience of orders and was eventually court-martialed. These charges came about as Colonel Albright encouraged his men to reject the discipline (and seriousness) of the state militia system. Albright's "Fantasticals," as they came to be known, paraded the streets during the Christmas holiday. He was escorted by a regiment of "Fantasticals" to his court martial hearing, and Albright watched sternly as men turned out in outrageous costume. Though short-lived, the Fantasticals Movement did spread to other locations in the United States.

Albright, oddly enough, was baptized a Roman Catholic at St. Augustine's Church on February 14, 1808, but he somehow became a bitter enemy of Catholics. He was such an ardent anti-Catholic that he sought to burn down the very church of his father (his mother was a Protestant), St. Augustine's, and to destroy the baptism register that held his baptismal record. He got his wish with the burning of St. Augustine's Church, but not before the registers were placed in the furnace in the basement of the church for safekeeping, thus surviving the inferno.

Colonel Albright owned a tavern on Second Street in the market house area of Northern Liberties, near Coates (Fairmount Avenue) Street. He kept a tablet at his public house to honor the dead of the Kensington Riots. The Irish had the practice of coming into his tavern daily and making insulting and abusive allusions about the tablet. On February 1, 1845, an Irishman by the name of John Clark entered the tavern and offered every indignity he could to Mr. Albright and then assaulted him in a "cowardly manner," inflicting several brutal kicks upon his person. Clark was arrested for his actions.

Like Lewis C. Levin and Peter Sken Smith, who both suffered terrible deaths by insanity, Albright also died an unusual death in the basement of a

wretched oyster house from "ulceration of the bowels." His death occurred on September 19, 1847, at age forty-one. His brother Jacob died in a fire in 1853, and his wife and daughter were drowned in 1856 in a sleighing accident on the Delaware River when the ice broke.

Courtyards of Irish Gunners

Out of curiosity, Edwin Greble rode up in a carriage in advance of the meeting and stationed himself in Second Street, opposite Harmony Court, where John Daley resided. As the meeting approached, he saw a number of armed men standing in and about the court, including Daley, who, as previously noted, was involved in just about every action that had taken place from May 3 through May 7. The first nativist demonstration Greble witnessed was four or five boys running out of the market house and attempting to kick in the hose house door. At this point, Daley and the armed men above deliberately leveled their guns and fired. They seemed to go up Harmony Court, load, run out toward the market and fire. Some fired where they stood. One man appeared to go "stealthily," as if hunting game. Unknowing to Edwin Greble, his brother Lewis Greble was shot down and killed at this time on Cadwalader Street. He was one of those attacking the hose house.

The group of Irish at Harmony Court, led by Daley, worked in conjunction with John Paul's group out of Weaver's Row. Daley's group would later also fire from the intersection of Germantown and Jefferson, from the northeast corner, peeking out from the corner, taking shots and then hiding again behind the corner building. They moved to this intersection from Harmony Court once Albright's men stationed themselves in the lot just above the north end of the market house, where they had a good view and aim on Harmony Court. With Daley were a number of men, among them James Sherry, Patrick Lafferty, David Funk and Peter Haughey. Sherry was heard to say that day, "I or we will kill all the damn sons of bitches we come across."

Albright, with about twenty men firing, caused the Harmony Court men to back off to Germantown and Jefferson, where they then began to pick off Albright's men one by one, until there was so many wounded that Albright had to retreat. It was at this time that Mathew Hammitt and Wesley J. Rhinedollar were shot and killed. Rhinedollar was shot as he rounded the corner at Cadwalader and Jefferson Street and started to head west. Hammitt was shot in the head at the same intersection, falling backward and

Looking west on Jefferson, toward Cadwalader Street, and the site where Rhinedollar and Hammitt were shot by Irish Catholics shooting east on Jefferson from Germantown Road and Harmony Court.

hitting his head on the curb at the northeast corner. Attorney B.F. O'Neill, who witnessed the shooting, stated that the man who killed Hammitt came out of McAfee's Court.

Besides the men at Harmony Court firing when the attack first took place on the hose house, John Paul and his armed friends (perhaps ten to fifteen men) farther north on Cadwalader began shooting at the nativists as well. The men would run out, go down the block a short distance, fire their rifles and then return to the courtyard, only to come out again and fire. It was done so quickly, it was speculated that they must have had a double set of rifles, with people loading the rifles for them, so that they could keep up a rather brisk firing at the nativists. As mentioned above, Paul had a box of rifles delivered to him that morning. Once Albright and his men arrived on the open lot above the market house, Paul and his men had to pull back some until Albright's men were thinned out and retreated.

The Beating of John Taggert

While the Daley and Paul groups fired many times, it was John Taggert who is credited with having been the first Irishman to fire his weapon on May 7 from an alley on Cadwalader Street, below Master. Taggert was a weaver, working for manufacturer Francis Brady, who resided around the corner on Germantown Road. Richard Walsh, another weaver, boarded with Taggert at the house of James Donohoe, yet another weaver, on the west side of Cadwalader Street, between Phoenix (Thompson) and Franklin (Girard). Taggert was observed to be especially active on May 7. He occupied a position in an alley where he would load his gun, venture to the end of the alley, take deliberate aim at whomever he saw within reach and fire; several times his shots were known to take effect. A man by the name of Maitland was dangerously wounded by a shot by Taggert. A "Negro" at the market shot at Taggert, and he was immediately shot in the forehead. There was a crowd of twenty or so spectators standing about at Master and Cadwalader, watching the action in front of the hose house. Taggert, assuming they were not combatants, tried to get through the crowd to get a better shot at the nativists. Unfortunately for Taggert, while perhaps not combatants, the spectators were nativists, with James Reddle and Bartholomew Baker being two of them.

At length, Taggert aimed his piece at James Reddle, described as an elderly man, and pulled the trigger, but the gun misfired and Reddle sprang forward, seizing him by the throat. Receiving assistance from Baker and some of the others, they secured Taggert and attempted to carry him to the office of Second Ward Kensington alderman Isaac Boileau to place him under arrest. The gun that was taken from Taggert was loaded ten fingers deep with powder and slugs.

Later in the year, at Taggert's October trial, Reddle stated that while on the way to Boileau's office, people followed and were beating Taggert along the way. Reddle stopped to get some "refreshments," leaving Taggert—apparently bound—outside, where the mob attacked him, beating him over the head with a paving stone. One person was heard asking for a meat cleaver to chop his head off. It was obvious from his testimony that Reddle did not care what the mob did to Taggert.

Taggert was eventually taken to Boileau's office, examined and committed to lock-up, but while being taken to prison, he was attacked again by a mob. Someone took the rope from Mr. Fagenbush's awning and placed it around Taggert's neck and drug him around while they looked for an appropriate place to hang him. He was strung up to a lamppost, where he begged for his life. He would have been left hanging but for the "interposition of some of the more humane of the people."

Taken down, he was dragged along the pavement some more and again severely beaten. Finally, the crowd left him for dead in one of the stalls in the market house in Second Street below Poplar, in Northern Liberties, apparently after beating him all the way from Kensington to Northern Liberties. It is said "thousands" gazed upon him, until one person noticed some life in him. He was then committed to the lock-up, where he was soon revived and placed in the hands of a physician who properly dressed his wounds.

Once Alderman Boileau saw Taggert, he could not tell if he was a "white man or colored." He stood mute, barely conscious. Five months after the riot, when Taggert first went on trial in October, he was still in horrible condition, and the judge threatened that "those who assaulted him would fare worse if they were before him, [as] it was a disgrace to Philadelphia." Eventually, Taggert was found guilty of riot, but the beating he took and the five months in jail since the riots was felt to be enough punishment, and he was not sentenced to prison.

The Retreat of Colonel Albright

Farther north on Cadwalader, one volley of gunfire from Paul and his men took effect on Lewis Greble, who was shot down, as was Charles Stillwell, both killed on Cadwalader Street. Peter Albright, the man that had helped Patrick Fisher and George Shiffler the previous day, was also on the scene when Greble was shot. Albright testified at a later trial that he saw Greble shot and attempted to carry Greble to his own house, but he died before he got there. He had been shot in the head through his hat, just above the brim, by John Campbell from a house at Cadwalader and Jefferson Streets. Later that night, when the rioting had subsided, Paul's house on Weaver's Row was searched and a case of rifles found. Paul was later arrested and charged with the murder of Lewis Greble on May 7, one of the first of the nativists to be killed when the mob attacked the hose house.

This testimony of Albright was not quite truthful. While he may have seen Greble killed and helped him off the field, it's rather doubtful that he carried him down to Northern Liberties where Greble lived. Rather, Albright was actually organizing a group of twenty nativists who, in military formation, worked their way north through the market house to an open lot at Jefferson Street, where

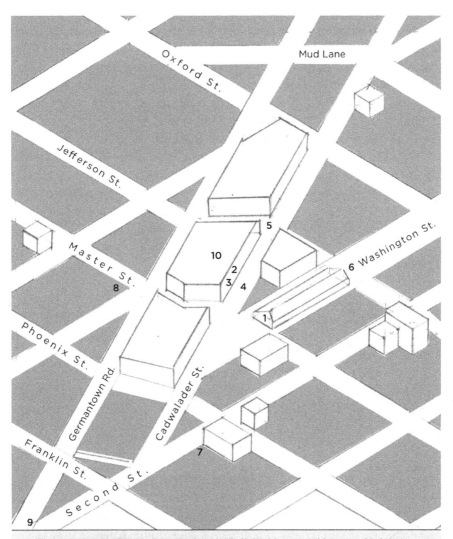

KENSINGTON RIOTS ON DAY TWO, MAY 7, 1844. Many neighbors packed their belongings and left their homes. After rallying at the State House Yard (behind Independence Hall), the mob of several thousand marched to Kensington. A smaller mob continued to the market (1). Several shots were fired from the Catholic houses (2). The mob attacked Hibernia Hose (3), then removed and destroyed the carriage. Greble, Stillwell and Young were shot (4). Hammit and Rhinedollar were shot (5). Albright was shot (6). The wounded included Augustus Peale, Peter Albright, Wright Ardis, William E. Hillman, James Whitaker, Charles Orte, Henry Heslepoth, Willis H. Blaney, John Lusher, and Mr. Lawrence. They were carried to Dr. Griffith (7) and the drug stores of Mr . Bower (8) and A.R. Horter (9). Ten or twelve houses (10) burned for several hours; escapees were fired upon.

A bird's-eye view of the second day of the Kensington Riots, May 7, 1844, with legend showing events and actions during the afternoon and evening. *Courtesy Torben Jenk.*

they took positions and laid volley after volley against the Irish at Harmony Court, Weaver's Row and Germantown Road and Jefferson Street. After firing, they would lay on the ground to reload so as not to be shot themselves.

Mary Whitman lived on Weaver's Row at this time, and at the trials later in the year, she described one Irishman who ran up to where she was standing by her house. He had broken his ramrod and stated he was "sure he had shot five or six, and he was sure the Lord was with him."

Within an hour of rioting, thirty nativists were more or less wounded, with at least four killed (Greble, Stillwell, Rhinedollar and Hammitt). The continuous discharge of the guns by the Irish drove the nativists from the ground, and the Irish continued shooting at anyone near enough to be shot at. Until after 6:00 p.m., the Irish had the ascendancy, and the Native Americans were shocked at the ferociousness of the Irish assault.

About 6:30 p.m., Albright, ex-constable of the Northern Liberties, was wounded in the hand. He left his position slightly north of the market house and moved to the southern end. Holding up his bleeding hand, he called on his friends to rally with him (there were many men watching the fighting from this vantage point). He returned to the ground with twenty or thirty men, all armed with muskets and rifles. These he organized and posted again just north of the market, where they fought for more than an hour. After Rhinedollar and Hammitt were killed and a number wounded, and with Albright himself already shot, his ranks were thinned and the group were finally forced to retreat.

ISAAC HARE AND THE DEATH OF JOSEPH RICE

While Albright was laying down fire from north of the Market House, several men took position on the east side of Cadwalader immediately in front of the buildings occupied by the Irish. They stood on the triangular lot, using several houses at the north end of the lot for cover, a well as a heap of gravel that was located near them. They let go a round of fire and soon attained a victory, as the Irish retreated. One of these men was young Isaac Hare who, while only a youth, was one of the bravest of the nativists and one of the leaders.

Hare lived on Third Street near Germantown. One witness stated at Hare's trial later in the year that he knew Hare well and talked to him on May 7, when Hare told him that the Irish were not fond of him or his family. The Hare family was the instigators of the riots: Isaac "Ike" Hare and his father, Nicholas, brought the nativist meeting to Kensington.

Burning of the Washington "Nanny Goat" Market on May 7, 1844, with militia watching. Hibernia Hose Company is also seen burning, the second building from the corner, on left.

James S. Funk was at the meeting at Independence Hall, where a man pointed Hare out to him and said it would be wise for Hare not to go to Kensington. Apparently Hare was well known by the Irish Catholics, and many were looking for him and his father. While the newspapers at the time state Isaac Hare was a teenager (seventeen years old), his baptism record shows that he was born in January 1821 and baptized at the age of four months on May 6, 1821, thus putting him at twenty-three years old during the riot. His parents were listed as Nicholas and Sarah Hare, and the baptism record lists the church as St. John's Methodist Church. The Reverend Busling performed the ceremony. Nicholas Hare was listed in 1850 as a manufacturer, age seventy-six, born in Ireland. There were other children. The family resided in Kensington's Third Ward.

Hare came up to Kensington with the mob from the State House Yard. James Donegan saw him with a gun on Second Street, near Phoenix (Thompson), with others. He started walking toward the market house and was quoted as saying, "Come on boys, don't be afraid, I will shoot the first damned Irish papist that I see."

Patrick Walls saw Hare from the second-story window of his house on Master Street, above Cadwalader. He saw Hare throw a stone against his door and yell, "Here is the house of another damned papist." The mob that Hare was leading also attacked the house next to Wall's. Edward Sheridan saw Hare at this time banging on doors and houses with his cane and told him to stop. A Mr. Hutchinson came up and also told him to stop, and Hare asked Hutchinson if he was a nativist. Hutchinson, an elderly Protestant, felt indignant that a boy would question him. He called Hare an "Irish son of a bitch and bastard." Hare ignored him, focusing on his march to the market house to shoot Irish Catholics.

Once at Washington and Master Streets, Hare, along with Solomon Vickers and Henry Haughey, worked their way up to the southernmost house on the eastern side of Cadwalader, between Master and Jefferson Streets. The triangular lot that sat between Cadwalader and Washington (American) had been used as a battlefield on both the previous day and this day. Hare and Vickers placed themselves here. Gunfire farther up on Cadwalader Street above Jefferson was aimed down at them. The fighting in front of the hose house had stopped at this point, and Hare and company did not have to worry about gunfire from the hose house, as it had been fired, and the houses next to it were already ablaze. The Irish on the southern two-thirds of the block had already been forced to flee.

It was at this time that Joseph Rice, an Irishman who doesn't appear to have been involved in the rioting but rather was hiding inside his house with his family, decided to peek out to see what was going on. Unfortunately for Rice, he was in plain sight of Hare and the others. All three men seemed to fire at Rice at the same time. Rice's home was on the west side of Cadwalader Street, not too far below Jefferson. A slug entered the right side of Rice's forehead, stopping in the back of his head after passing through his brain. From the wound, his brain was oozing out: he literally had his brains shot out.

Rice had been inside his yard; his wife told him not to go out, but he went anyway. A Mr. Schaeffer, on the next lot (south of Rice), told Rice that the house below him was on fire. Mr. Schaeffer told Mrs. Rice to keep the children upstairs, as Rice had gone outside to see how close the fire was to his own house. Bridget Rice and their two children, nine and eleven years old, were frightened. She went downstairs to tend to some bread she had been baking. She opened the door and called to her husband when Mrs. Develin, another neighbor in the courtyard, said, "Joe has been shot."

Rice was found lying in the yard, feet against the fence, shot in the head and apparently falling backward, feet still to the fence. He breathed for about an hour and died. The Rices' house did not cover the whole lot; they had a yard front and back and an alley beside it. Rice was shot in the front yard, standing on an elevated area of the yard, which allowed him to see over the fence. Rice was fifty-seven or fifty-eight years old.

Constable Sanders Gavit of the First Ward Kensington would later testify at Hare's trial. Gavit had seen Hare earlier in the day, gathering with others at Phoenix (Thompson) and Second Streets, where they were organizing with guns. There were others who would not go themselves but who furnished guns to the ones who did go to the market house. Gavit went over Phoenix to Cadwalader, and the mob with Hare went up Second to Master and then on to the market area. Hare was in the lead of the mob, and Gavit saw him shoot his gun up Cadwalader Street. Several men with Hare also fired. One was above him and one below him, just above Master at the market, all firing toward Cadwalader or Jefferson and Cadwalader. Solomon Vickers, nicknamed "Texan Bill," was one of the men. They laid their guns on the fence to give them better aim and remained there two or three hours. Gavit had seen about fifty people armed but only knew about half a dozen of them; even though he had lived in Kensington thirteen years or so, he had only been the constable since the previous spring.

Rice's house sat back from Cadwalader and the front door opened toward McKee's house, with a passageway between the homes of McKee and Rice. Schaeffer's brick house was connected to Rice's on the other side. Hearing the mob approaching and learning of the shooting and killing at Jefferson and Cadwalader, Schaeffer and Rice went out to see for themselves, walking up to the corner and seeing Hammitt's blood on the pavement. Both had returned home when Schaeffer's brother-in-law also came home and said the house below them was on fire. Schaeffer climbed out on the roof of his shed to view the fire when he saw a man on Cadwalader Street above Jefferson pointing a gun at him. He jumped down from the roof. Rice had been in the yard, arms folded, looking over the fence. After Schaeffer jumped off the shed roof, he went into his house and heard no more of Rice until he heard he had been shot.

Besides Joseph Rice and his wife, Bridget, and their neighbor Mr. Schaeffer and his brother-in-law, there were also four other people holed up in the small courtyard where the Rice house was situated. Jane Develin, one of Rice's tenants for four months, rented a house that was connected to Rice's. She lived there with another woman and two children. On May 7, she, the other woman, the children, Bridget and Joseph Rice and Schaeffer and his brother-in-law were all waiting for a break in the rioting so they could escape.

After Rice was shot, Bridget Rice grabbed her husband's wrists and tried to drag him into the house, screaming out for help. Develin helped her and then packed some things and took off for the woods, where she stayed all night. Henry McGraw came as well to help with Rice, and with Bridget, they wrapped Rice's head with wet cloths. Rice had never had a gun that day.

Attorney C.B.F. O'Neill, a Catholic, had witnessed Hammitt's death earlier. He took sick of the sight and went home (Fourth Street near Master). He later testified that he came back out to the riot area and saw a number of people on the open lot between Cadwalader and Washington (the triangular lot). Some of those gathered on the lot had firearms, and there was considerable firing from a party in Cadwalader Street, above Jefferson (Paul and Daley's men), and another party occupied Cadwalader Street below (Taggert and others), as well as groups in the lot (Hare and his men) and the market (Albright's men). The first party (Paul and Daley's men) had command of Germantown Road and Cadwalader above Jefferson. There were five parties on the ground. Some of the houses on Cadwalader were on fire. Hare, Haughery and Texan Bill were on the empty triangular lot, north side, by the brick buildings, when they shot Rice. There was a pile of building stones in the street on Cadwalader between Master and Jefferson, where a man (probably Lewis Greble) was shot dead and carried away.

Testimony showed that Hare was an active participant on both May 6 and 7 and appears to have been one of the worst spirits among the rioters, a ringleader of the mob on Monday, who led the attack on Quin's house in Master Street ("Come on boys") after the meeting was fired on. He, with his shotgun, was seen organizing an armed group at Phoenix and Second to go back and fight. He and Vickers were the most exposed of any of the combatants. Other witnesses testified that Hare was seen previously on Monday, with a pistol, throwing brickbats. He tried to shoot people who were throwing stones at him, but the gun didn't fire. Frances Rex, of Charlotte Street, knew Hare and saw him on Monday throwing stones on the triangular lot. He saw a man break open John Carroll's house on Cadwalader and set it on fire.

John Gorman stated that Hare and the others all had guns with bayonets on them. He saw twenty or thirty of them. He stated that they marched four abreast, with Hare in the middle of the front line. He thinks Hare was nicknamed "Ike." One witness, William Buck, testified that he saw Hare with a club busting open doors of houses on Cadwalader Street.

Francis Weiss, a carpenter who resided on Fourth Street below Master, was standing at his shop door facing Charlotte Street on Monday, May 6, looking toward Germantown and Master. At the riot trials, he testified that he could see Hare, who acted as a leader of his party, encouraging the men to fight on. He could not see the Irish, as they were farther north on Germantown.

The ruins of the Nanny Goat Market (Washington Street Market), only the pillars remained. Other damage to neighborhood seen in background.

Soon the Irish came back down Germantown with guns firing, scattering the Native Americans, and he saw Shiffler shot and staggering before being led off. Hare had previously been standing at the intersection of Germantown and Girard with his club over his head, waving it and telling his fellow nativists not to be afraid. Weiss was at Cadwalader Street the following day when he saw Rhinedollar holding the tongue of the Hibernia Hose carriage; later on, Rhinedollar was shot dead. He knew Rhinedollar, and it made him sad to see him shot. Weiss also saw the hose house go up in fire. He saw Hare go up with a gun in his hand, peeping in an alley; he stayed there until the fire got going good and then went over to the triangular lot, where he stood still for about fifteen minutes until someone yelled "Look out!" He then moved about and took runs toward the hose house, fired, moved toward the mob and then went out of sight. About a dozen men were firing up Cadwalader Street, with about eight or so men firing back from Harmony Court and Cadwalader Street. The witness watched from Cadwalader and Master. At that point, it was too dangerous, and Weiss walked toward his house on Fourth Street. He stayed at home on the advice of a Mr. Clark (probably Hugh Clark). Weiss was an apprentice to Charles Clark, brother of Hugh Clark. He was twenty years old.

When the hose house was fired, it went unchecked due to the rioting. While the shooting continued up and down Cadwalader Street and back and forth on Jefferson Street, the hose house fire spread to the adjacent buildings. The Irish were unable to try to put out the fire; if they did, the nativists would shoot them. In all likelihood, the Irish escaped through the back alleys and courtyards to Germantown Avenue. In a short time, every house on the west side of Cadwalader Street between Master and Jefferson that had had a gun shot from it was on fire.

John McKee, Joseph Rice's next-door neighbor, testified that he lived in a brick house, adjacent and south of Rice on the west side of Cadwalader. When he heard the nativists were coming, he went to his third floor with a man named Bartholomew Johnson. He saw three men (Hare, Vickers and Haughey) come up to the triangular lot and make a stand there, looking farther north (toward Harmony Court above Jefferson). One man tried to fire out from behind the first house on the north side of the lot, but when he went out, he was met with fire that McKee saw hitting the bricks of the house the men were hiding behind. Haughey then left, leaving Hare and Vickers. One of the men waved his hat out past the edge of the building to have the Irish fire at it, which they did. He then went back behind the building, and one of them put the gun to his eye and fired toward Rice's house. The shooter then slapped his knee and said, "I got my man." They then went away. McKee knew Hare and said it wasn't him, so it must have been Vickers who shot Rice, as they both appear to have fired at the same time, but Haughey was also charged with the Rice murder. The homes of McKee and Rice were both in the court, and their front doors faced each other, not Cadwalader Street. McKee's house sat twenty-eight feet off Cadwalader Street. Schaeffer, McKee and Johnson all packed their goods and left.

Mrs. Catharine Storm testified at Hare's trial. She stated that after the meeting was broken up on May 3 by the Catholic party, she went up to put the children to bed. When she went up, the windows were open and a party of Catholics were gathered on the next step. They pointed out Isaac Hare, Mr. McManus, Mr. McMurray's son and several others that she was not acquainted with. The Irishmen then expressed their determination that the Natives should not hold a meeting in that ward; the words they used were, "The Orangemen should not hold a meeting there, that all they wanted was to make Orangemen of the Natives." Terry McDonald said that if Gee had given his house to the Natives to hold a meeting, he and the others would not have left one stone upon another. This mention of Orangemen, along with the fact that the nativists sang the Battle of the Boyne song when St. Michael's Church's cross on the steeple came crashing down, plus the fact that the nativists were flying an orange flag at one point, all go to show that a number of the nativists were indeed Orangemen, and their battle with the Irish Catholics was a continuation of the battles they had fought for many years back in Ireland.

Mrs. Storm told McManus the next day what she heard, and he said there would be a meeting on Monday, May 6. She went to the meeting, and when it started to rain, she went home. Climbing up to the third story of her house, she watched the excitement from her window. Later, she went out to get one of her children and saw Hare get hit in the back of the neck by a stone thrown by another boy.

Witnesses at Hare's trial testified that there was firing from a blue frame house next to Rice's. One witness even went so far to say that they saw Rice with a gun, poking it through the fence, but didn't see him shoot it, so perhaps Rice wasn't innocent after all.

Hare was found guilty of murder in the second degree and laid upon the mercy of the court by the jury due to his youth. It might be that the defense played up Hare's youth—even falsifying Hare's age, perhaps—in an attempt to get him a lighter sentence. It worked. Hare was not sentenced to prison, as evidence was more convincing that Henry Haughey was guilty, which he was, and he was subsequently sent to prison. "Texan Bill" (Solomon Vickers), the other accused of the murder of Rice, escaped to New York, where he was arrested and escaped from jail, only to be locked up again in Philadelphia and sent to trial, where his case was dropped.

By this point, those who were killed by the Irish and the order they were killed included:

- Lewis Greble, of Fifth and Christian, who died instantly from a bullet entering his right temple and passing out the crown of his head. Like Joseph Rice, he too had his brains blown out.
- Charles Stilwell, a twenty-three-year-old ropemaker from Fifth and Carpenter, was shot dead on the triangular lot between Cadwalader and Washington, not far from the hose house. He was shot from a yellow house, which was soon fired. He had been standing with his hand in his pocket. He was said to be doing nothing, but this area was the hottest area for the rioting, so he was surely involved.
- Soon after Stilwell's death, Wesley J. Rhinedollar was at this same location on the triangular lot and, after moving up to Jefferson Street, was shot in the back. Right after this, there was a rush on the stable where Taggert was captured. Rhinedollar, of Front and Green Streets, had been shot in the back right shoulder, with the bullet passing out of the left side of his chest.

- Mathew Hammitt, of Allen and Crease Streets, died instantly from a shot in the ear. He too was at the intersection of Cadwalader and Jefferson Streets. He was the nephew of the noted Kensington shipbuilder John Kile Hammitt.

George Young, of South Street, was at first thought to be fatally shot. He was shot in his chest near the hose house, the ball passing out his back near the shoulder blade. Fortunately, he somehow managed to live and later testify at the riot trials.

Several years later, when the Mexican War broke out, Isaac Hare volunteered. He is listed as a lieutenant in the Second Pennsylvania Volunteers, where he again showed his bravery but also showed his darker side. Hare and Benjamin F. Dutton, also of the Second Pennsylvania Volunteers, with Lieutenant Bryant P. Tilden of the Second U.S. Infantry and an unnamed gambler were spared the hangman. They were charged by the military for breaking into a gambling hall (Calle de la Palma) late at night in Mexico City on April 5, 1848. When the owner appeared, one of them shot him in the head and killed him. Evidence and testimony showed that Hare was the leader of the group. These sorts of crimes happened, but very rarely were officers involved. They were all to be hanged to set an example, but by late May, the Americans were evacuating Mexico and Major General William O. Butler spared them.

Lieutenant Hare of Company F, Second Pennsylvania Regiment, sent a letter back home to his family from his commanding officer, praising Hare's bravery. The family had the letter published in the *Philadelphia Inquirer* on February 26, 1848:

> *Hare was serving under Capt. Naylor's Philadelphia Rangers and was in command of the company at San Angels. His conduct throughout the whole campaign had been meritorious. A call went out for a storming party to lead the assault on the strong fortress of Chapultepec. Hare was one of the first to volunteer in this perilous enterprise. His conduct at the storming of the fortress was such as to command the admiration of his fellow officers, and to draw from me in my official report a high commendation of his gallantry. To merit distinction among so many brave officers and men, reflects upon him the highest credit.*
> —*Maj. Gen. J.A. Quitman, U.S.A., late Comd'g. Vol. Div.*

The letter to his family was also published, which stated in part:

City of Mexico, March 30, 1848, at present we are stationed at San Angel, a delightful spot, some nine miles from the "Halls of Montezuma," about which so much has been said and written. Our company numbers about twenty-five men at present, who are all principally in good health.

BURNING DOWN THE HOUSE: THE KILLED AND WOUNDED

After Greble and Stillwell were killed at the outset of the shooting, Mathew Hammitt and Wesley Rhinedollar were also killed a short time later when the action moved farther north to Jefferson and Cadwalader. During the trials later in the year, several witnesses—such as George Friheller, John McCleary and Peter Kenney—all stated that they saw Hammitt killed and that John Daley and his men were the shooters.

Hammitt was at the intersection of Cadwalader and Jefferson with his gun pointing up Cadwalader Street, ready to fire at John Paul and his men at Weaver's Row. At this time, several shots were fired at Hammitt from the party of Daley's men at Germantown and Jefferson. After missing him twice, one of Daley's men at Jefferson and Germantown knelt down and took deliberate aim with his gun at a rest, hitting Hammitt as he was coming across Jefferson and Cadwalader. Hammitt fell dead. As he received the wound, his tarpaulin hat flew off, and the ball penetrated his brain, passing through his ear. When he fell, his head hit the pavement at the northeast corner of the intersection. When the witnesses saw Hammitt lying in the street, Hammitt had his gun lying across his chest. Some tried to carry him away, waving handkerchiefs. The men who shot Hammitt allowed them to pick up the body, but someone from Paul's group took a shot at them, shouting, "Leave him lie." They dropped the body and ran off. Friheller and McCleary came back later and dragged the body away.

While it appears obvious from testimony that Mathew Hammitt lost his life by gunfire from the party at the corner of Jefferson and Germantown, William Shields, one of the commonwealth's witnesses, certainly threw some doubt on this otherwise clear statement. He says he saw Hammitt coming up Master toward Cadwalader street with a gun in his hand and that he advised him to stay away, but Hammitt refused, saying he would "stick it to them." Shields stated that Hammitt fell at the corner of Jefferson and Cadwalader Streets, with Shields standing in Cadwalader Street, only ten feet below

Jefferson when Hammitt was shot. Shields also said he saw Hammitt shot from a blue frame house in Harmony Court by a short man in a frock coat, with a black hat on. He stated that before Hammitt was shot, Hammitt fired his gun up Cadwalader Street.

Besides the deaths, many nativists were wounded—too many for an accurate count, but it seemed to be at least thirty. A Mr. Lee was shot and wounded, as was John Broadhead, who was struck on a coat button by a spent ball and stung in the face with some small shot. C. Salisbury was shot and wounded. Willis H. Blaney, late high constable, was shot in the heel and badly wounded. Washington Agberger was also badly wounded, and ship carpenter Wright B. Ardis was shot through the hip. John Lusher of Shackamaxon Street was shot in the left side of his chest. An elderly man named James Boggs of Allen Street was shot in the arm. William E. Hillman was shot in the left shoulder. A young boy named Smith was shot and wounded. Henry Hesselbaugh, a tavern keeper at Third and Poplar, was shot in the hand. Charles Orte was shot in the head but lived. A man named Keyser and another named James Whitaker were shot and wounded. Thomas Funston was shot in the head but not killed, and a man named Maitland was shot by Taggert. S. Abbot Lawrence of Boston, a spectator, was struck in the chest with a ball from a gun but was saved from injury when it made contact with a piece of money in his pocket. John Shrieves, a painter from Front and Green, was shot in the head and thought to be killed, but he survived. John S. Fagan was shot in the shoulder. John Sutter had a ball enter his left breast, inflicting a terrible wound. Another young man, passing by on his way home from work, was shot and wounded badly. A man named Andrew Gates and another named Yocum were wounded. At least four young boys were also shot during the rioting, and unnamed others were wounded as well.

Augustus Peale, a dentist and ardent nativist, was shot in the arm. He lived in the lower part of the city (100 block of Lombard) and was struck above the middle of the arm, the slug passing through the limb with extensive laceration of the soft parts, producing "a frightful comminuted fracture of the humerus, the bone being splintered so far up as to make it necessary to amputate very near to the shoulder." He later testified at the trials that he remained in the market house for about fifteen minutes, all the while it was being fired into. On leaving, he went into Cadwalader Street, where one ball passed close to his ear; another through his fingers; a third struck his hand, but its force being spent, did him no injury; and a fourth struck his left arm, splintering the bone to such an extent as to require immediate amputation, thus maiming him for life.

A.R. Hortter's drugstore at Edward Street and Germantown Road was used Tuesday night as a sort of medical clinic to care and dress the wounded of the riots. A number of others were also taken to a drugstore owned by a Mr. Bower at Germantown Road and Third Street, and still others were taken to the residence of Dr. A.E. Griffiths, on Second Street, below Thompson Street, where they were attended to by Drs. Bethel, Duffield and Griffiths. These three places acted as field hospitals for the nativists during the battles of May 6 and 7.

On the Irish Catholic side, it is difficult to determine all the killed and wounded. An Irishman by the name of Johnson was seen killed in a house on Cadwalader Street. As mentioned previously, Joseph Rice, an Irishman, was shot in the head and killed as he peaked over his fence. An Irishman was said to be killed at the corner of Jefferson and Germantown, but not until he had discharged several muskets at the nativists. He was, it was reported, shot through the back of the head. A history of St. Michael's Church, written in 1934, states three bullet-riddled bodies were found in the yards of the Irish. Eyewitnesses and newspapers reported that upward of seven or eight other Irish may have perished in the fires, afraid to come out for fear of being shot down. On May 9, 1844, it was reported, without substantiation, that several families—including men, women, children—had perished on Tuesday,

May 7 in the burning houses. Still later, on May 12, an Irishman was found dead among the ruins of the houses on Cadwalader Street. The several families said to perish in the fires and the single man found in the ruins may have been the seven or eight thought to be burned up in the fires. In total, there may have been upwards of fourteen or fifteen Irish Catholics killed, probably higher. The real number is not known.

Robert McQuillin (1834–1910), arrested as a boy for participation in Kensington Riots, later served honorably in the Civil War and local politics. *Courtesy Elizabeth Clark.*

The nativists were exposed and put up a good fight, but every time the Irish let loose a large discharge from the houses on Cadwalader Street, their ranks were felled greatly. Several nativists were able to make their way to the northwest corner house at Master and Cadwalader Streets, occupied by a Mrs. Harris, who fled, leaving her life savings of $700 behind her. The nativists fired her house, and the fire spread to the adjoining houses. When the other fires were started, the Irish Catholics on Cadwalader Street were forced to flee, going out the backs of their houses, hopping over the fences of their neighbors one by one until an opening allowed them to escape to Germantown Road or to Cadwalader Street. As the Irish came out into the open, the nativists attempted to shoot them down. About ten to twelve houses were on fire at this point, including the Hibernia Hose Company. Except for Rice and Johnson, the Irish dead were lost to history. Eventually, the entire block of houses on the west side of Cadwalader between Jefferson and Master was on fire, including some on the adjoining block of Master. Several nearby fire companies tried to enter the area to put down the fires but were driven off by the mobs.

The Military Arrives in Kensington

Convening with his military officers of the first brigade on Tuesday morning (May 7) at Military Hall on Library Street, General George Cadwalader became convinced of the need to call up the militia. At about 1:00 p.m. on Tuesday afternoon, Cadwalader issued orders for the full assembling of the whole military force of the first brigade. He had viewed the rioting on Monday night with Sheriff McMichael and personally saw Ramsay and Wright shot down as the nativists attempted to assault the nunnery and the Irish defended it. The sheriff did not want to call out a posse, as the rioters were too numerous and too well armed, offering the advice that only the military could put down the rioters. Cadwalader agreed with Sheriff McMichael. Cadwalader himself was under the command of Major General Patterson. Colonel Lee acted as an aide to Cadwalader.

Arriving at about 9:00 p.m. on Tuesday evening, Captain Hubbell's Jackson Artillerists (approximately fifty men) and Captain Tustin's National Guard (approximately thirty men) were ordered to stand guard at the intersections of Master and Washington (American) Streets, Master and Cadwalader and Master and Germantown Road. An accompaniment of soldiers positioned two fieldpieces loaded with grape and canister at each end of the market, to protect for any activity that might confront them from Jefferson or Master Streets. These two military groups stayed the entire night, being relieved on Wednesday, May 8 at about 8:00 a.m. by Captain Small's Monroe Guards (approximately forty men) and the Philadelphia Cadets of Captain White (approximately thirty-five men). It must have seemed odd for General Cadwalader to have to post his men on Cadwalader Street, a street named to honor his family.

What was left of the Irish Catholics' personal possessions were still in their burned homes. A nativist newspaper gave the following description of the battlefield as the military arrived:

> *There is now an alarm of fire, which it is said is near the field of battle, and the confusion attending upon it, the vociferation of the firemen, and ringing of bells in the upper districts, the carrying away of the dead, the groans of the dying, the shouts of the Americans, and the yells of their enemies, the rolling of the drums of the military, all conspire to render a scene at once exciting and terrific to the stoutest heart. A number of the military being beset by the enemy, fled in all directions. We were unable to designate which company it was, but we are informed that it was for the want of ammunition and guns.*

The presence of the military almost brought the rioting to a complete stop. The military's arrival also allowed the firemen to come in at about 10:00 p.m. to commence putting out the fires, which took until almost midnight. The Carroll Hose Company and the United States Engine Company were quickly on the scene, to be joined later by several other fire companies from the city and adjoining area. The fires were unchecked for several hours, and when the firemen arrived, upward of thirty buildings were burning or already consumed, both north and west of the market house, while the 260-foot-long Nanny Goat Market, which caught fire from cinders from the burning houses, and the Hibernia Hose Company were nothing but ashes.

Having heard rumors that St. Michael's Church was occupied by armed men who were storing ammunition there, General Cadwalader made an inspection of the church, finding the rumors to be untrue. He did, however, take possession of St. Michael's Church to ensure it wouldn't be fired, stationing guards at different positions around the church.

Tuesday's rioting had more than seventy-five armed nativists who dared to enter into the bloody arena of Washington and Master Streets. The rest, numbering from five thousand to eight thousand, blocked up every avenue and street leading to the market house. In all likelihood, the Irish may have had a similar number of actual combatants, or perhaps slightly less. As soon as the armed men appeared in front of the Irish houses along Cadwalader Street, volley after volley was fired into them. The fire was returned, but with little effect, as the Irish Catholics were sheltered, for the most part. This battle lasted over an hour, during which at least thirty-two nativists were shot, with four killed. At least two Irishmen were known to have been killed, and upward of twelve to thirteen others were either shot dead or burned alive in the fires. A number of Irish were wounded, but it is not known how many, as they did not seek help for their wounds with the local authorities for fear of being imprisoned for participating in the riots (like John McAleer, who found this out the hard way the previous night when he was arrested at a hospital seeking help for his thumb that was blown off when his gun misfired).

Besides firing houses, the nativists began searching homes looking for arms. Mrs. Malone testified at the later trials that she saw the meeting arrive between 4:00 and 5:00 p.m. and that some of the men, armed with guns, pushed her down on the front pavement's cellar door and broke into her house, inquiring for arms and asking her if she would die for her religion. They said they would "shoot her husband to inches, if they had him, but would not hurt a woman." Finding no guns, they went away.

A number of Irish Catholics fled their homes after the buildings started to be torched by the nativists. While some left on Monday, May 6, many were still trapped in their homes on Tuesday due to the rioting going on outside and the streets filled with nativists. However, when the torching of their homes began, they had no choice, and when the military arrived they had protection. They fled to the nearby Camac's Woods. From a contemporary account of the riots, published as *A Full and Complete Account of the Late Awful Riots in Philadelphia*, we find the following:

> *No less than two hundred families have been compelled to remove from their homes…Men with their wives, and often six or seven children, trudging fearfully through the streets, with small bundles, seeking a refuge they knew not where…a large number of Irish Catholics and others, who were so ruthlessly thrust from their homes during the riots had encamped in Camac's Woods and other places, some two or three miles north of the city…They were without food, except what chance or charity threw in their way, and destitute of clothing sufficient to protect them from the damp night air. While in this deplorable situation one woman gave birth to a child.*

Camac's Woods is described as being located north of Berks, west of Tenth Street, surrounding the mansion house of Turner Camac (Eleventh and Montgomery) on both sides of Broad Street. Honorable George M. Stroud, judge of the district court and whose house stood near Camac's Woods, with several other residents of the vicinity, did all in their power to help the displaced Irish Catholics, but there were so many of them that Judge Stroud had to call the attention of Paul Reilly, an officer of the court, to the distressed condition of the refugees. Mr. Reilly, who lived in St. Patrick's Parish, hired a furniture car and, with the assistance of several other generous Irishmen in the neighborhood, loaded it with meats and bread and blankets, and thus provided for the poor people who had taken shelter in the woods.

Reporters covering the riots for the *Philadelphia Inquirer* on Tuesday night reported seeing bodies being carried from the field on sofas.

> *The sufferers exhibited sights of a truly heartrending kind, their wounds bleeding, and their clothes dyed in blood. Dozens of families, nay hundreds, were flying throughout the day and evening, from the scene of peril, some in one direction and some in another. Among them were old men and old women, mothers with little children, boys and girls,—all excited and panic-stricken. The burning houses, with their lurid flames, presented after nightfall another fearful feature of the scene.*

By 1:30 a.m., with the military patrolling the streets of West Kensington, the second day of rioting finally came to an end. After the firing of the neighborhood, the advantage surely swung in the nativists' favor. Too many nativists were either killed or wounded to give them an outright victory in round four of the riot, but with the Irish being chased out of the neighborhood by the burning of their houses, the riot was certainly tipped to the nativists' favor.

CHAPTER 7

WEDNESDAY, MAY 8, 1844

THE THIRD DAY OF RIOTING

As daybreak approached and with military protection, many Irish families that had feared to leave on Tuesday now took the chance. Carters were kept busy loading the possessions of families into their carts, taking with them as much as they could carry. Parties of men and women, both young and old, and with children, set off for Camac's Woods or parts unknown. By all accounts, it was a very sad scene of human misery.

The Jackson Artillerists and the National Guard were still on duty as the morning of May 8 arrived. These two groups stayed the entire night, being relieved on Wednesday morning at about 8:00 a.m. by Captain Small's Monroe Guards and the Philadelphia Cadets of Captain White.

Some military guards could be seen posted around the body of Joseph Rice, the Irish Catholic who was shot down by Isaac Hare and his men the previous evening. His body was laid in the yard of his house. Some insisted that he was not involved in the riots. Rice's only offense was being curious, peering over the fence of his yard when he was shot in the head. His body laid where it fell the whole night, with his wife and two children mourning by his side.

As the morning progressed, large numbers of people came to see the devastation of the night before. A good many of the onlookers were nativists who came to loot and hunt for any Irish homes that still had guns. Self-organized bodies of men were formed, and searches were conducted throughout the houses, chiefly the houses from where the Irish had fired their guns during the previous two days (on Cadwalader, Jefferson and Master Streets). Even outhouses and a pigsty that sat behind the houses on

Cadwalader Street were searched. Some guns were found and confiscated, and the military rushed in to protect the property of the vacated Irish Catholics. There were several stands of arms such as rifles, muskets, shotguns and pistols that were found concealed. They were almost all loaded.

At around 11:00 a.m., groups of mostly boys who had been active in pulling down the walls and chimneys of the burned-out buildings were joined by young men near the homes where some of the Irish had shot from the previous day. Soon the back of a row house fronting the burned market on Washington (American) Street caught fire, and the Irish Catholics who lived there were forced to flee. This was at the row of houses on the west side of Washington Street, at the upper end of the triangular lot where much of the previous days' fighting had taken place. The fire alarm went out, and a hose company came to extinguish the fire but needed the security of the Monroe Guards to protect them.

Other men searched a nearby house for hidden firearms. They were cleared out by the military, but twenty minutes later, the home went up in flames. The fire spread to five frame houses that were attached to it, and they were all lost. By noon, the crowds of nativists and their supporters had begun to grow and become unruly. With the protection of the military, many of the Irish Catholic tenants of the homes along Cadwalader Street, Master Street and Washington (American) Street and the various courts and alleys coming off of these streets were busy packing their belongings and fleeing the neighborhood. As the Irish moved out of their homes, the houses were soon fired by the mob, and in minutes a whole row of frame houses on Harmony Court were in flames, as well as several three-story brick buildings at Jefferson and Washington Streets and another on Washington. Harmony Court, as was previously stated, acted as the headquarters for the Irish the previous day.

The military appeared helpless as nativists crept under cover from alley to alley firing any Irish Catholic houses they came upon, regardless if they were occupied or not. Any property from which gunfire had emanated during the previous two days was especially targeted. As a group of military would head to one location, the nativists would fire another building a short distance away. By keeping this up, they had the military running in circles.

Oliver Cree, an Irishman, was taken from his house on May 8, somewhere near Cadwalader Street, in which were found two loaded muskets. He was taken from the hands of the officers and beat most unmercifully, after which he was taken to the mayor and placed in lockup. Cries rang out in the crowd: "Hang him, hang him!" However, the police were able to make it to the lockup, where the accused was detained.

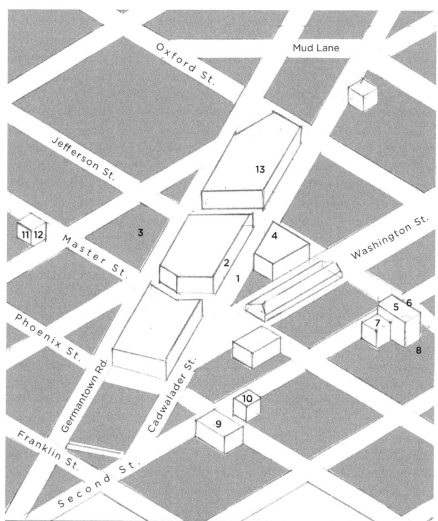

KENSINGTON RIOTS ON DAY THREE, MAY 8, 1844. Rice found dead (1). Seven or eight tenants found dead (2). Pig sty demolished (3). Those "searching for arms" and valuables set new fires in the attics houses, then fled (4). Captain Fairlamb inspected St. Michael's Church (5) for weapons and took the keys. Father Donohue left under the protection of the military. Fairlamb went on patrol and by noon the church was set on fire along with the Priest's dwelling (6) and small frame dwellings (7). Women stood behind trying to guard their possessions. A couple buried their infant in the churchyard (8). The Female Seminary (9) was set on fire and became a heap of ruins. Corr's Temperance Grocery Store (10) was completely riddled and everything inside was destroyed. Rioters gutted homes of Alderman Hugh Clark (11) and his brother Patrick (12). Six or eight houses in Harmony Court (13) were set on fire as the Philadelphia Grays and Junior Artillerists arrived.

A bird's-eye view of the third day of the Kensington Riots, May 8, 1844, with legend showing events and actions during the afternoon and evening. *Courtesy Torben Jenk.*

At about 2:00 p.m., a large nativist mob went to Ninth and Poplar Streets, where a great number of Irish had taken refuge. The houses were set on fire and the Irish driven out. Eventually, many wound up camping with the other refugees at Camac's Woods.

The Firing of St. Michael's Church, Rectory and the Nunnery

The first two days of rioting saw the Irish Catholics with the upper hand, shooting from the cover and safety of their homes. In this way, a small number of men were able to keep a much larger body of nativists at bay. However, all that changed once the nativists began to fire the houses, forcing the Irish out into the streets. Vastly outnumbered, the Irish retreated. On the third day (May 8), the nativist mobs returned, determined to finish what they originally set out to do: to burn down St. Michael's Church and rid Kensington of its Catholicism. As they patrolled the neighborhood firing what buildings they could, the cry finally went out, "On to St. Michael's," and the rush toward the church began.

Earlier in the day, at about 10:00 a.m., Father Donaghoe, the original pastor of St. Michael's who was visiting from Iowa (he was no longer the pastor of St. Michael's, as Father Loughran had taken over when Donaghoe moved to Iowa to be with the Sisters of Charity), had left St. Michael's under the protection of the military, taking a carriage to St. Augustine's Church, leaving Father Loughran at the rectory. Later, after St. Michael's was fired, Donaghoe watched the fire from the steeple of St. Augustine's, little knowing that church would also later be fired.

At about 2:00 p.m., a crowd gathered on Second Street near the church. They at first started to pelt the church and rectory with stones and brickbats and missiles of every kind, and the military stationed around the church made no attempt to stop the mob. The Wayne Artillerists (between thirty to fifty men), Monroe Guards, Lafayette Guards (approximately forty men) and Independence Rifle Corps (approximately twenty-five men) stood watching.

Once the mob gathered outside the church and rectory, Father Loughran gave the keys for St. Michael's Church to Captain Jonas P. Fairlamb of the Wayne Artillery Corps, whose men examined the church, found no arms and locked the place up for safety. With the help of the military, Loughran boarded a carriage and was escorted by the military with some difficulty through the crowd and away from the area. Unbeknownst to Donaghoe and Loughran, the front door of the church appears to have been left unlocked by Fairlamb's men. Historians argue if it was done on purpose or not. The majority of the military at this time were Protestants, so it would not be a stretch to think some sympathized with the nativists, a complaint raised by many Catholics after the rioting was over. It would certainly explain the military's inaction in putting down the mob during the time they were stationed in Kensington and its taking action as the rioting shifted to the city proper, where the Protestant patricians lived. Another factor for the initial inaction of the military in Kensington was the uncertainty of the military as to whether they indeed had the authority to shoot down citizens if they were not attacking the military. If the mob was attacking property and not the military, did the military have the right to shoot them down?

A Philadelphian by the name of H. Loomis wrote to his brother in Oran, New York, on May 9, the day after the riots, expressing his thoughts of the inaction of the military:

> It seems impossible for the military to do any thing for if they had fired they would of killed hundreds of innocent people not only this, but I found there was but one feeling they were all for killing and destroying the British [Irish] Catholics…the Americans continue their havoc all day yesterday and all night last night. They destroyed and broke all their furniture, smashed up bureaus, secretaries, looking glasses, carpets, and every thing you can think of, of the best kinds of furniture, had a fire on the street and burned them, they burnt down 2 churches, R.C., the handsome edifices I most ever saw…I can assure you there is not an Irishman to be seen in this city at this time or yesterday, if they had been seen, they would [have] all been killed.

While the mob was outside the church, several small fires were lit in nearby houses. A detachment of soldiers was sent to those locations, leaving the church thinly protected. At about 2:30 p.m., someone entered the church and set a fire in the entryway. It quickly spread to the rest of the building, and before long the entire church was on fire. Another frame house on the south side of the church was also fired. The flames soon were shooting out the windows of the church, with the steeple engulfed in flames. With the help of the wind, the flames were communicated to the adjacent priest house and other houses on the block, and before long, just about the whole block was on fire. Several houses owned by a Mr. McCreedy were destroyed, as was the Second Street Sugar Refectory, owned by McCreedy. Furniture, books and other items were

Burning of St. Michael's Church by the nativist mob on May 8, 1844. The church, rectory and neighboring properties were all destroyed.

Burning of the Sisters of Charity Nunnery/Seminary (southeast corner of Phoenix and Second Streets) by the nativist mob on May 8, 1844.

thrown from the buildings, and the mob gobbled them up. The rectory was looted. In all, the church, rectory, two factories and five houses on the block were all burned to the ground. Several fire companies came to put the fires out but were helpless, as the mob would not let them near the fires. While the church burned, the rioters yelled, screamed and danced in the streets.

While the church was ablaze, an infant was being buried in the graveyard behind the church. With Father Donaghoe and Loughran having fled the mob, the only ceremony for the child's burial was the prayers of the parents, drowned out by the crackling timbers of the fired church. During the burning of St. Michael's Church, when the cross at the peak of the roof fell, the mob "gave three cheers and a drum and fife played the Boyne water," a reference to the song commemorating a Protestant victory in Ireland at the Battle of the Boyne where Irish Catholics were defeated in the year 1690. Some of the mob made a celebratory march into the cemetery behind the church, mutilating and knocking over the tombstones.

By 4:00 p.m., the destruction of the church and rectory was complete. Now the attention of the mob was turned to the nunnery down the street at Second and Phoenix (Thompson) Streets, the only thing left of St. Michael's buildings. As they approached the building, now vacated, they tore down the wooden fence that they had previously attempted to fire on Monday night. Men entered the building, breaking out the windows and tearing off the shutters, and lit fires in various areas of the building. Before long, the nunnery was aflame. The military, still positioned at the destroyed church, now hurried down to the nunnery, but it was too late: the building was totally torched and burning.

Corr's Temperance Grocery Store opposite the nunnery was attacked next. This was revenge for Monday night, when Irishmen fired at the nativists from the roof of the building, killing Ramsay and Wright, who were with the mob attempting to fire the nunnery. The military stood by and watched as the store was battered, looted and gutted of its contents. Another brick building at this intersection was also fired.

The Arrival of General Cadwalader and Colonel Page and the End of the Riot

Soldiers of the First Brigade, under the command of General Cadwalader, arrived in Kensington at about 5:00 p.m. The troops approached the riot area from Fourth Street. At Fourth and Franklin (Girard), they separated into two groups: one under the command of Cadwalader and composed of the Philadelphia Grays (approximately fifty men), with two pieces of artillery; and the Junior Artillerists (approximately fifty men), with one or two other companies of the First City Troop (approximately twenty-two men) in front. This first group proceeded over Franklin (Girard) to Second Street. This intersection had acted as a staging area for the nativists during the rioting of May 6 and 7. The other group (the State Fencibles), led by Colonel James Page, continued up Fourth Street to Jefferson and then went over Jefferson to Second Street to St. Michael's Church. The mobs at first thought to challenge the guards, but the artillery of the National Guard was enough to change their minds. Page personally dismounted and, with his life in danger, entered the mob and appealed to them, as Americans, to disperse. After some tension, they agreed, gave Page three cheers and retired. In Thomas South Lanard's *One Hundred Years with the State Fencibles*, Colonel Page is quoted on what happened:

> *A detachment of volunteers, under the command of Col. Joseph Murray, was sent in advance to Kensington. Reaching that place, it took a position in the neighborhood of the disturbed district, and while there, received information that the rioters had attacked, and were then gutting a store in Second Street. Colonel Murray immediately put his command in motion, and on reaching Second Street, wheeled to the right in column of sections, when a terrible scene presented itself. The whole street, something more than a square below, was filled with rioters in hot pursuit of some of the Sheriff's posse, who were flying for the [their] lives in the direction of the advancing column. I saw, at a glance, that there would be a conflict between the military and rioters. I suggested to Colonel Murray the necessity of occupying the whole width of the street by forming platoons, and thus protecting his flanks, which he promptly did, (halting his command and preparing for the onset), and telling him of my purpose, I advanced a considerable distance in front of the column, waving my sword in the air to attract attention, directing the fugitives to take refuge behind the military, and shouting to the rioters to stop or they would be fired upon. My object was to divert the mob and avoid a collision. In an instant I was surrounded by hundreds of them—the rush in the direction of the military stopped—the flying officers escaped—a new object presented to the mob. There was a pause, and a bloody catastrophe averted. Although they crowded around me, heard what I had to say, and provided me with a stand from which and shut me out from the column and all aid, and made use of coarse threats, they offered no violence of any kind, but wanted to speak,*

Alderman Hugh Clark's house (next to corner) and his brother Patrick's house (corner) before ransacking by the mob on May 8, 1844.

which I gladly availed myself of... They listened to me patiently, dropping away and thinning out by degrees, until the whole scene, an hour before so full of violence and terror, became comparatively quiet.

The Protestants of Kensington came to love Colonel Page and later named their literary institute on Girard Avenue the Colonel James Page Library.

As the mobs began to filter out of Kensington, they continued to fire and destroy buildings along the way. Once such building was the home of Alderman Hugh Clark, a leader of the Irish Catholic community and perhaps one of the wealthiest men of Kensington. His was the second house on the west side of Fourth Street, south of Master. The corner property was his brother Patrick's tavern and home, which at one time had a dye house in the rear. The mob ransacked the homes, cutting open the beds, scattering Clark's papers and notes, breaking out his windows and destroying his furniture and library. His brother Patrick's property met the same fate.

When the military arrived at Clark's house, the mob moved on to Patrick Murray's store at the southeast corner of Jefferson and Germantown Road. Murray had helped the Irish on Tuesday, supplying ball and shot and other items to the Irishmen. For the mob, this was reason enough for the destruction of Murray's store, which was sacked, looted and burned. As the military then raced to Murray's house, several of the rioters returned to Clark's house to enact further destruction.

With more and more military arriving, the mob was sufficiently put under control. While some lingered, many began to drift downtown toward St. Augustine's Church, and so ended the third and final day of rioting in Kensington. The nativists had completed what they came to do. They destroyed the Catholic neighborhood in West Kensington and its institutions, scattered its residents and burned it down to the ground. Round five was a knockout victory for the nativists.

CHAPTER 8

THE AFTERMATH

The author has tried to provide the details of Kensington's Nativist Riots, an event that is probably the most cited event in all of Kensington history. He has not dealt at all with the ensuing riots that broke out in July 1844 by the nativists, as those riots took place in Southwark and, while interesting, were outside the scope of this story. A number of lives were lost and scores wounded in Southwark.

When enough destruction was wreaked on Kensington and there was nothing left to burn, the nativists set their sights on other Catholic churches in the city. It is said that some went to Fifth and Girard, where St. Peter's was being built, but there wasn't much enthusiasm to fight with Germans, particularly when they were armed. A march into Philadelphia to St. Augustine's Church was the next target. Here the mob crowded around the church at Fourth and New Streets. A small number of soldiers guarded the place. Mayor Scott of Philadelphia mounted a carriage to speak to the mob, trying to talk sense to them, but there was no sense for the senseless. The mayor was hit in the chest with a rock and soon left the area.

The initial group of National Guards was driven away from St. Augustine's by an assault with stones and brickbats. This allowed the building to be entered, supposedly by a fourteen year old, and set ablaze. The main body of the military was still in Kensington, guarding the ashes of the ruins of that neighborhood. Other groups of soldiers were hurriedly stationed at St. Mary's on Fourth Street and St. Joseph's on Willing's Alley, both below Walnut Street. Other soldiers were stationed at St. John's Catholic Church

Nativists riot with militia in Southwark (today's Queen Village), July 1844, several months after the Kensington Riots. St. Philip de Neri Church shown in background.

Illustration taken from *Awful Riots*, showing the burning of St. Augustine's Church by the nativists on May 8, 1844.

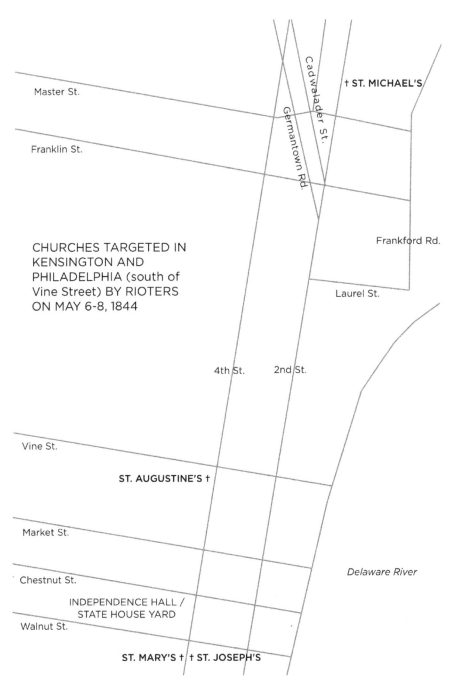

CHURCHES TARGETED IN
KENSINGTON AND
PHILADELPHIA (south of
Vine Street) BY RIOTERS
ON MAY 6-8, 1844

Master St.

Franklin St.

Cadwalader St.

Germantown Rd.

† ST. MICHAEL'S

Frankford Rd.

Laurel St.

4th St.   2nd St.

Vine St.

ST. AUGUSTINE'S †

Market St.

Chestnut St.

Delaware River

INDEPENDENCE HALL /
STATE HOUSE YARD
Walnut St.

ST. MARY'S † † ST. JOSEPH'S

St. Michael's and St. Augustine's, Catholic churches targeted by nativists, were fired, but St. Mary's and St. Joseph's were protected by military and saved. *Courtesy Torben Jenk.*

on Thirteenth Street, where the mobs began to gather. Seeing that the military might actually start to take action when the rioting spilled over into the city proper, the crowd didn't dare to advance on those churches. With a military that was finally ready to act, the mob retired and the Nativist Riots of May 1844 finally came to an end. However, the military needed to stay on duty for a number of days.

St. Augustine's Church was burned to the ground, along with its rectory and academy. Several neighboring buildings caught fire as well, and a very valuable library was looted from the rectory, its contents piled into the street and made into a celebratory bonfire. A. Warner Erwin, a Philadelphia conveyancer, wrote the following thoughts in his journal on May 8, 1844:

Went up to the office and remained there through the day and evening until about ½ past 9 o'clock, when there was an alarm of fire, and having heard some rumors of the mob intending to set fire to St. Augustine's Church (Catholic) in 4th St. opposite New, wended my way in that direction. About ½ past 9, fire was communicated to the vestibule of the Church, it is said by a boy about 14 years old. It increased with rapidity when once under way, and dense masses of smoke curled out from every window. In a few minutes the flames reached the belfry, and burst out from the upper window in broad sheets. The whole steeple was soon wrapt in the devouring element, and presented a terrific yet grand aspect. The clock struck ten while the fire was raging at its greatest fury. At 20 m. past 10, the cross which surmounted the steeple, and which remained unhurt, fell with a loud crash, amid the plaudits of a large portion of the spectators. Ten minutes afterwards the steeple, which had stood until burnt to a mere skeleton, fell throwing up a mass of cinders which fell like a shower of gold on the Building & Streets northeast of the church. The heat during the height of the fire was so intense, that persons could hardly look at the flames at the distance of a square, and the light was so brilliant as to dim even the gas lamps. Besides "St. Augustine's," St. Michael's Church and nunnery and a number of houses were burned this afternoon, and the mob, it appears, has had virtual possession of the county of Philadelphia for the last two days and nights, and the law has been defied with impunity. Lives and property have been sacrificed in a desperate and terrible conflict, and anarchy and riots, amounting almost to civil war, have obtained a power and boldness which is without parallel in the history of our State. Well may it be asked with regret, and apprehension, what will be the ultimate result of such a fearful state of things? Are our liberties to be surrendered to the rash and headlong domination of mobs, or are we to fly from this greater evil to the lesser one of a consolidated military police? To one or the other of these extremities we seem to be rapidly approaching, and, unless the moral atmosphere of our city be thoroughly purged, we must be content to suffer all the horrors of sanguinary tumults, reckless invasions of right and liberty, and a blind and indiscriminate destruction of property, or submit to be [dragooned] into an obedience to the law. An awful responsibility rests with those who have caused and promoted these calamities, and are yet stimulating to their continuance and their reward must and will be the abhorrence of all good men and the anathema of every patriot.

George W. Ziegler, a visitor to Philadelphia, stopped by the site of St. Augustine's four months after the riot. In a letter written September 1, 1844, to his wife back home in Greencastle, Pennsylvania, he gave the following grim view of the church:

This morning Mr. Smiley and myself walked out to see the ruins of Saint Augustine's Church. It is an awful sight to look upon, there is nothing remaining, but the front and two side walls, with a portion of the back wall, all that could be burned by fire is destroyed, there is not even a door or window frame remaining. It is the very picture of desolation. It seems almost miraculous how the adjoining houses were saved. It is surrounded by buildings on all sides and is in the very heart of the city. If I get any leisure time I intend to visit the ruins in Kensington.

At least nine nativists were arrested and charged with arson and riot for the burning of St. Augustine's; however, only two of them appear to have served any time.

After the 1844 riots of May and July, the Nativist Party exploded. From a small group of about five hundred before the riots, it grew to have supporters in the tens of thousands. In the November elections of 1844, the party won three of the four congressional seats for Philadelphia and sent nine men to the state legislature. The following year, the nativists captured the municipal government of New York City and Philadelphia, including winning six commissioner seats for the District of Kensington. Lewis Levin was among Philadelphia's new nativist congressmen. He was reelected two more times, becoming the most prominent national figure in the party during the 1840s.

On the afternoon of May 27, 1844, the Native Americans had a meeting on the corner lot at Second and Master in Kensington, the site of the original meeting where the riot first erupted. The meeting was called to order, speeches were made, resolutions passed and everything was conducted with "strictest propriety," ensuring that no disturbances occurred. Of course, the Irish had been burned out and probably had yet to come back, thus there was no opposition left in the West Kensington neighborhood. After the riots, nativists had regular meetings in Kensington, including a celebratory one-year anniversary meeting on May 6, 1845, again at the lot at Second and Master Street. The day before this one-year anniversary, Kensington's Board of Commissioners passed an ordinance that established a police force, with a superintendent and forty officers, eight officers for each of the then five wards. Kensington's Third Ward, the Irish Catholic neighborhood, had no officers with recognizably Irish surnames.

On August 7, 1844, the ship *Native American* was launched from Van Dusen's yard in Kensington. There were ten thousand on hand to watch the event, many of them members of the Nativist Party. There was a large rally with speeches. Later in the month, on August 31, 1844, the Native American Party met near the Old Bridge in the Fifth Ward. The frigate *Native American* was anchored at Gunner's Creek, decorated with flags and streamers, illuminated from stem to stern and firing salutes. Jacob Moser was appointed president, addresses were given by General Peter Sken Smith, Wm. Hollingshead, H.L. Smith, John Perry, Wm. Deal Baker, G.W. Reed and Peter Albright. A band played.

On December 6, 1844, the *Philadelphia Inquirer* announced that Mrs. F.S. Henry, of 155 South Tenth Street, was said to execute works in human hair that formed small pictures for breastpins and the like. She finished one of a large size with the hair of the Native Americans killed in Kensington. It exhibited much patient industry.

The Irish didn't take the popularity of the nativists sitting down. On July 19, 1844, a body of some two hundred or three hundred Irishmen surrounded the house of Mr. Sands, a former Native American candidate for constable of Cedar Ward. Three men went in, brought Sands out and beat him nearly to death. This took place in the southwest section of the city near the Schuylkill. In another incident, Thomas Kelly was held to bail by the mayor to keep the peace on Saturday, July 20, 1844, on the charge of using threatening language immediately after the Kensington Riots. He was heard to say that there was no military protection for the Irish Catholics, and if any more churches were burned, the Irish would attack the Fairmount Water Works and fire the city. Alderman Hugh Clark brought suit against Wm. D. Baker and H.H.K. Eliott, editors and proprietors of the *American*

Advocate, a nativist newspaper, and charged them with libel. George Emery attempted to drive through the nativists' meeting on September 19 in Northern Liberties and was arrested and charged with assault and battery on J.M. Goodwin.

In January 1845, a newspaper ran the following story. John J.N. Douglas, captain of the nightly watch for the District of Southwark, was arrested and charged with assault with intent to kill. He was held on $2,000 bail. Douglas went into a grocery store at the corner of Third and Shippen (Bainbridge) and went up to John Smith, who worked there, and stated, "You are a Native American—make a short prayer—I am going to shoot you." Smith, realizing Douglas was serious, ran into a small counting room, closing the door after him. Douglas discharged his pistol at him, the ball passing through the door and falling on the floor of the room Smith had taken refuge in.

Besides still defending themselves, the Irish went about rebuilding their neighborhood. On August 9, 1844, it was announced that the houses that were lost during the Kensington Riots at the corner of Master and Cadwalader were starting to be rebuilt. Later in the month, on August 26, it was announced, "There has not been for many years past such improvements in the District of Kensington as during the present season. In every quarter almost new buildings, of good style, are being put up. On the site of the great conflagration, during the riots, two new brick house have been put up, two more are nearly up, and several others are under way." Work on the Nanny Goat Market began almost immediately and it was put back into use, though it was soon closed by the District and moved to Franklin (Girard) Street. St. Michael's Church had a temporary chapel built and was opened for service within a month of the riot. The new permanent church had its cornerstone laid in August 1846 and was dedicated in February 1847.

The Combatants and the Killed and Wounded

An estimate of the active participants in the riot on May 7 is not easy to pinpoint. Newspaper reports and trial testimony state that between sixty and seventy-five hardcore nativist rioters were actually armed and involved in the most violent aspects of the riots. While the mob swelled to several thousand, it is likely only several hundred actually took part in the rock throwing, house burning and rabble-rousing and in general acted as the "the mob."

A nativist song sheet, dedicated to "American Republicans" and showing the supposed "tattered flag" clutched by George Shiffler as he died.

W. S. & J. CROWLEY,
BOOKSELLERS AND STATIONERS,
146 Baltimore Street.—Wholesale Ag'ts for Baltimore.

George Shiffler

☞ *It will be remembered that this young man was shot on the 6th of May, 1844, in the Kensington Riots, by a Band of Foreigners*

Americans, attention give,
  I'll sing a solemn lay,
In memory of a much loved one, } REPEAT.
  Slain on the Sixth of May.

He was his mother's only son,—
  The Widow's heart is sore,
She weeps, she mourns that he is gone,
  GEORGE SHIFFLER is no more.

Cut off in all the prime of youth,
  This noble young man fell,
Slain by a ruthless Foreign Band,
  Hark! hear his funeral knell.

" I die, I die," he nobly said,
  " But in a glorious cause,
In exercise of Freedom's Rights,
  My Country and her Laws."

Although he's dead he speaks aloud,
  Americans to thee,
Arise! Columbia's sons, arise,
  In all your majesty.

Protect your Country, and her Laws,
  Come to the Rescue, come,
We'll put all Foreign influence down,
  Arise! Protect your Home,

Our Flag's insulted, friends are slain,
  And must we quiet be!
No! no! we'll Rally round the Flag,
  Which leads to Victory.

Printed and for sale at G. S. HARRIS'

CARD AND JOB PRINTING OFFICE

S. E. cor. 4th & Vine Sts., Phila.

Contemporary nativist broadside, containing a poem dedicated to George Shiffler, the first person killed during the Kensington Riots, slain by a "ruthless Foreign Band."

The numbers of armed Irish Catholics who were actually involved in the hardcore rioting were probably of a comparable number to that of the nativists, with perhaps upward of sixty who actually took up arms to defend their neighborhood against the invading nativists. Most of these men lived on Cadwalader Street or the adjacent streets to it. A number of them lost their homes in the riots. Many other Irish Catholics simply became involved because their homes were being attacked or used for cover by fellow Irishmen.

In reading through the literature of the Kensington Riots, authors have focused on the main nine people who were killed, those whose names are known. These nine men were George Shiffler (age nineteen), Joseph Cox (age twenty-three), William Wright (age nineteen), Nathan Ramsay (age twenty-one), Lewis Greble (age thirty-two), Charles Stillwell (age twenty-three), Wesley Rhinedollar (age nineteen), Mathew Hammitt (age thirty-seven) and the Irishman Joseph Rice (age fifty). However, only the eight nativists are held up as martyrs, their names emblazoned on flags and monuments and used in songs and poems. On the Irish side, the names of the Catholics (besides Rice) who were killed in the riots are lost to history. Of these eight nativists, only one—Hammitt—actually lived in Kensington. Ramsay, Rhinedollar, Shiffler and Wright were from the Northern Liberties, with Cox, Greble and Stillwell coming from Southwark. Many of the wounded were also from Southwark and the Northern Liberties. Isaac Hare was from Kensington, but Peter Albright was from the Northern Liberties.

With a deeper reading of the historical record, we find that the three days of rioting in May 1944 in Kensington resulted in at least twenty-three or twenty-four killed, though there were most likely more. Besides the eight nativists, the Irish that were killed were Joseph Rice; a man known only by the name "Johnson;" two bodies found in the ruins days after the riots; and an Irishman who was reported to have been shot and killed at Cadwalader and Jefferson. There were three bodies found in the yards of the houses on Cadwalader Street that were riddled with bullets, as well as the reported seven or eight people burned up in the buildings.

The casualties are low estimates, particularly for the Irish wounded, as Philadelphia officials and newspapers at that time were not keeping track of Irish Catholics wounded, nor were the Irish reporting them. As a fairly new immigrant community, they were somewhat insulated from the Protestant society at large. Days after the riots ended, authorities were still pulling bodies from the burned Irish Catholic homes. Many of the wounded Irish did not seek help from the authorities or local hospitals, so it is impossible to determine the number of casualties they actually suffered, but the thirty-nine nativists reported wounded would appear to be rather low for them, and the numbers for the Irish were not even counted.

The Destruction in Kensington

The arena of the Kensington Riot was the rectangle that stretches from Perry (Palethorp) Street west to Fourth Street and from Franklin (Girard) Street north to Oxford Street. This area was in St. Michael's Parish, the heart of Irish Kensington in the nineteenth century. The destruction of property during the Kensington Riots is fairly well documented. The loss of property was considered in the hundreds of thousands of nineteenth-century dollars. In today's dollars, it would be millions.

St. Michael's Church, at Second and Jefferson Streets, was destroyed, as well as all the buildings associated with it. The priest's rectory next to the church and houses on the south side of the church were destroyed. The nunnery located at Second and Thompson Streets was burnt to the ground. Other public buildings associated with Kensington's Irish Catholics were also burned down, such as the Hibernia Hose Company on Cadwalader Street and the 260-foot-long Nanny Goat Market that sat in the middle of Washington (American) Street, north of Master. The market was the home to Irish life in early Kensington.

Upwards of sixty Irish Catholic homes and stores were burnt to the ground. These fired buildings were located along the north side of Master Street between Germantown Avenue and Cadwalader Street, the west side of Cadwalader Street, between Master and Jefferson Streets and along the west side of the upper block of Washington (American) between Master and Jefferson Streets. An entire row of frame houses on Harmony Court, which sat off of the west side of Cadwalader, above Jefferson, was also destroyed, as well other homes along that block. Homes were also damaged on Second Street near the intersections of Phoenix (Thompson) and Master, and many homes on Second Street above Franklin (Girard) were stoned and battered. The homes of Alderman Hugh Clark and his brother, at the corner of Fourth and Master Streets, were ransacked but spared firing due to their vicinity to residences of Native Americans.

The appendix at the end of this book gives a list of properties that were recorded as being destroyed by fire or otherwise damaged during the Kensington Riots. This list is compiled from various contemporary accounts, both newspaper reports and published histories of the event. It does not include the buildings along Second Street between Franklin (Girard) and Jefferson Streets that had their windows, doors and furniture smashed and destroyed as the mob marched up Second Street.

THE CIVIL TRIALS

The calculations that were available for the monetary losses did not include, for the most part, the contents of the buildings. It was estimated that with St. Augustine's Church, losses were upward of $250,000. Calculated in today's value, it would be in the neighborhood of tens of millions.

The *Public Ledger* reported on October 16, 1844, that there were twenty-nine people who were seeking damages from the county for losses suffered during the riots. Besides the ones listed in the appendix that did win damages, the following individuals also sued the county for damages: John Mallon, Patrick Conway (Washington above Jefferson), John Dougherty, Michael Masterson, Bridget Clark (Hugh Clark's mother, who lived with her son), W.&J. Browning (Cadwalader above Master), Elihu Pickering (owned land on Washington Street, between Master & Jefferson), James Traner (Germantown above Master), John Beatty, William Browning (Cadwalader above Master), John McBride and Owen McCulla.

George Mifflin Dallas and Henry Phillips, the attorneys who defended the Irish Catholic rioters against the Commonwealth in criminal trials, switched sides and worked for the county for the civil cases when the Irish Catholics sued the county in district court to recover their losses. In all, there were between sixty and seventy civil suits against the county.

THE CRIMINAL TRIALS: PHILADELPHIA QUARTER SESSIONS COURT, MAY 1844–JANUARY 1845

The Kensington Riot trials began almost immediately in Philadelphia's Quarter Sessions Court, May Term of 1844. However, the bulk of the cases were held for July and then pushed back until September, as time was needed to gather all the witnesses. They would not be finished until 1845. The cases caused a great stir in Philadelphia, as they were probably the most exciting trials in Philadelphia history up to this point. John Daley's case was the first homicide case to be tried and attracted a great deal of attention due to the "investigation into the doctrines of the common law, respecting riots and unlawful assemblies." All over the country, many watched to see how the riot cases would be played out in the Philadelphia courts. One newspaper reported, "So important were these trials considered, that three judges would preside, to give all the parties the benefit of a full Court in the discussion of the many legal points that are expected to arise. Such a session of any Court never before was held in the Commonwealth, or indeed in this Union."

The prosecutors and defense attorneys were all well-known attorneys in mid-century Philadelphia. For the Commonwealth, there was Ashabel Green Jr., J. Murray Rush and attorney general Ovid P. Johnson. For the defense, Attorney George Mifflin Dallas helped to defend John Taggert, John McAleer and John Daley. Dallas became the Democratic vice president of the United States in 1844 under President James K. Polk. Perhaps his work with the riot trials was a pitch for the Irish Catholic vote, which tended to vote the Democratic ticket. Also working with Dallas on Taggert's case was William Axton Stokes (1814–1877), a known Philadelphia attorney. On McAleer's case with Dallas was Henry M. Phillips (1811–1884), a Democratic attorney who served one term in Congress in the 1850s. David Paul Brown also worked with Dallas and Phillips on Daley's case, one that brought much attention nationwide. David Paul Brown (1795–1872) was part of a small group of Philadelphia lawyers, who as members of the Pennsylvania Abolition Society, tended to represent African Americans (both free and enslaved). Brown was also the attorney for Patrick Murray, along with Stokes. Brown, Stokes, Phillips and Robert G. Dodson all helped to defend John Paul against his murder charge.

For the nativists, Peter A. Browne (1777–1860), from an old prominent Kensington and Northern Liberties family, represented Isaac Hare, helping him get off on his murder charge of Joseph Rice. Joseph S. Brewster, a known nativist attorney, and E. Coles Lambert were also Hare's attorneys, and they also worked some of the other cases for the nativists.

There were at least sixty-five people arrested during the riots in Kensington. Of these, twenty-five were nativists and forty were Irish Catholics. These individuals had their cases heard by the Quarter Sessions Court in over forty different trials during the course of several terms between May 1844 and January 1845. Between the Commonwealth and the defendants, there were about 186 witnesses who testified, many of whom lived in the area of the riots and witnessed the fighting or were actual combatants themselves. They consisted of both Protestants and Catholics.

The court cases show that the Commonwealth stated that there were more than one hundred other people who were active in the rioting, but their names were unknown and they, therefore, could not be arrested, charged or put on trial. Of the cases that made it to the court, the Irish Catholics appeared to have been found guilty more often than the nativists, which was to be expected in a city where municipal offices were filled with Protestants.

On the nativists' side, seven men were charged with arson. George Aberrick was charged with arson of St. Augustine's, and the outcome of his trial is unknown. Young Frederick Hess was found guilty of arson and given one year in Eastern Penitentiary. John Pasot, Walter Allen, Robert Cochran and John Coulter all had their arson cases heard together. They were charged with burning and damaging St. Michael's and St. Augustine's churches, but their cases were ignored by the court. John McKeown was charged with arson of St. Michael's Rectory but found not guilty. There were fourteen nativists charged with riot. John Bennett was arrested while in Moyamensing Prison. He was charged with being engaged in the riot at the nunnery on May 8. Bennett was in jail for beating Constable Gavit with a club the previous night on Oxford Street, as Gavit was in pursuit of him at the time for knocking down a woman. A Protestant John Daley was arrested on the charge of breaking into the nunnery with an axe at the time it was destroyed by fire. Henry Andrews was arrested and charged with being concerned in the destruction of the Hibernia Hose Company. James Merrick and Henry Ganges were charged with rioting at St. Augustine's. The outcome of their trial is unknown. Thomas Gansey was charged with riot but was committed to the almshouse because his intellect was impaired. George P. Bonin's case was ignored by the court, as was that of Joseph C. Dayman; John Hess pled "nolo contendere," or no contest. Josiah Nickels was found guilty and sentenced to two months in jail. Timothy Croney was found guilty. Peter Albright was found not guilty, and Isaac Wilson Taylor's charge was ignored by the court. He was the man who sacked Hugh Clark's house. Joseph Fow was charged with breaking into McGee's house on Washington Street and battering it. Isaac Hare was also charged with riot, but the charge was changed to murder. There were also three nativists charged with murder. Solomon Vickers, Isaac Hare and Henry Haughey were all charged for the murder of Joseph Rice. Vickers's charge was ignored by the court, and Hare was found guilty but placed at the mercy of the court due to his age. The court, in turn, pardoned him. Henry Haughey, on the other hand, was found guilty of murder in the second degree and sentenced to two years solitary confinement at Eastern Penitentiary. One man was charged with a misdemeanor for mutilating tombstones in the cemetery: David Becket. He pled guilty and received a sentence of four months in the county prison.

For the Irish Catholics who were caught and arrested, there were thirty-five men and one woman charged with rioting. John O'Neill was found guilty and given nine months in county jail. Edmond "Ned" Sherry was found guilty and given three years in prison. Terence "Tarry" Mullin was found guilty and given three years in prison as well, but he was later pardoned. He had been seen smashing an old man in the head with a stone. Thomas Wall and John "Little John" Lafferty were found not guilty. John Paul was originally charged with riot, but the prosecutor changed it to murder. John Riley and James Fitzpatrick were found not guilty. Riley supposedly shot George Young in the chest, the ball going right through and nearly killing him. Robert McQuillan, a young boy who was not yet a teenager, was found guilty of throwing stones and sentenced to an amazing one year in the county prison. It might be added that up to 50 percent, if not more, of the rioters on both sides were teenagers. John Currey was found not guilty, and John and Patrick Holmes had their charges ignored by the court. John Taggert, who took a horrible beating, had his riot charge changed to murder. Store owner Patrick Murray was found guilty but later pardoned. A man known only by the name of "James" had his riot charged ignored. Others charged with rioting but whose outcomes are unknown were Margaret Lafferty, John Heinsell, Hiram McVey, Patrick Wall, John McIldown, John Runnahan, John Forsyth, Oliver Purip, Thomas Dougherty, Patrick McDonough, Patrick Campbell, Owen Dailey, John Donnelly, John O'Connor, Thomas McWilliams, David Funk, James Lawson (who was shot in both legs), John McAleer (who lost his thumb when his gun misfired), Bernard Sherry and Patrick O'Neill. James Sherry was arrested for riot, but the charge was changed to murder.

There were also six Irishmen charged with murder. John Campbell was charged with the murder of Lewis Greble, and his outcome is unknown. Hugh Develin was charged for the murder of Charles Stillwell, and his outcome is also unknown. Develin was also charged with shooting Augustus Peale, the man who lost his arm. John Taggert was originally charged with the murder of George Shiffler, but the charges were dropped. John Daley's sensational case for the murder of Mathew Hammitt found him guilty of murder in the second degree and sentenced to four years solitary confinement at Eastern Penitentiary. John Paul was found guilty of murder in the second degree of Lewis Greble and was likewise sentenced to four years solitary confinement at Eastern Penitentiary. James Sherry was charged with the murder of Wesley J. Rhinedollar, and his case was pardoned. Two men, Francis Small and Alexander McDonell, were said to have actually been the shooters for Shiffler (Small) and Greble (McDonell), but they supposedly escaped back to Ireland. A grand jury produced twenty witnesses who testified to the fact that Small and McDonell were the shooters.

The Kensington Riot combatants, the deaths, the wounded, the destruction and the court trials are all nothing but a memory, but those memories lived on for several generations in the neighborhood. Old-timers sitting at their local Kensington taprooms told stories, and the oral history of the riots was handed from one generation to the next. When McClure, Phillips & Co. published John T. McIntyre's novel *The Ragged Edge* in 1902, almost sixty years after the riots, McIntyre's characters—Kensington residents—made several references to the riots. McIntyre himself was born in Kensington in 1870 and was a member of St. Michael's Parish, thus he was sure to have heard those stories from the old-timers in the neighborhood. *The Ragged Edge* is a novel about Irish ward politics in Kensington, and early in the book there is a dialogue between two older Irish Catholic women who recall the Nativists Riots:

> *In the kitchen of a squat, shabby building fronting on the railroad, a lean, yellow-faced old woman sat beside the range, nursing her knees and drawing at a black clay pipe. Another, almost her counterpart, was sweeping the floor with the worn stump of a broom.*
>
> *"God be good till uz, Ellen!" suddenly exclaimed the first. "What are yes about?"*
>
> *"What talk have ye, Bridget?"*
>
> *"Sure ye wur as ner as a hair till swapin' the bit av dust out av the dure!"*
>
> *"Divil a fear av me. Is it swape the luck from the house I'd be doin?"*
>
> *Ellen scraped up the sweepings. "There do be bad luck enough about the place," she continued, as she slid the dust into the fire and watched it burn, the flame lighting up her old, faded face, her dirty white cap, her bony, large-veined hands. "Malachi tells me that the biz'ness do be poorly."*
>
> *"Little wonder," declared Bridget, knocking the ashes from her pipe and laying it carefully on the top of a tin at the back of a stove. "I know'd what 'ud come av havin' the son av a Know-nothin' glostern' about the place! Sure the curse av God is on the loike!"*
>
> *"True for yes," assented her sister. "Owl Larkin wur the spit av the owld felly himself; he wur a Derry man an' as black a Presbyterian as iver cried "To h—l wid the Pope!"*

Ellen took up the hot pipe and charged it from the tin, shaking her head ominously.

"Ah, the Orange thafe!" piped the other. "Well do I remember him, years ago, at the riots at the Nanny-Goat Market, that stood beyant there where the railroad is. Sure it wur him that put the devil in their heads till burn down St. Michael's; an' wid me own two eyes I see him shoutin' an' laffin' as the cross tumbled intill the street!"

Ellen made a hurried sign of the cross and muttered some words in Gaelic.

"An they say," whispered she, awed, "that he barked loike a dog iver after!"

"Sorra the lie's in it, avic. Owld Mrs. Flanagan, that lived nixt dure till him, towld me, wid her own two lips, that it wur so. Bud he always said it wur asthma he wur after having."

"Oh the robber! It wur himself that cud twist t'ings till serve his turn. More like it wur the devil in him, crying' till be let out."

"An'd' yez raymember at the toime av the riots, Ellen, whin he stood be the fince, overight our back yard, wid Foley's musket, waitin' for any av uz till pop out our heads?"

Ellen, through some mischance, had swallowed some of the rank pipe smoke, and she gasped and strangled, with waving hands and protruding eyes. "Well do I, asthore," she panted between her fits of coughing. "Oh, the Crom'ell!"

Like McIntyre's novel, today the riots are just a memory, a story of long, long ago. The Kensington Riot was an important event in Philadelphia's history, as the devastation helped the leaders of the city see that consolidation of the county was necessary, particularly for policing reasons. The riot helped to push for the consolidation of the county into the city in 1854. Another outcome of the Nativist Riots was the formation of the parochial school system, instrumented by then Bishop John Neumann, later St. John Neumann, of St. Peter's Church. This helped to settle the Bible question for the Catholics. Even LaSalle University was soon born from the ashes of the Nativist Riots; it was originally located on Second Street, across from St. Michael's Church.

List of Property Damage of Nativist Riots, May 6 — 8, 1844

Twenty-Two Buildings on the West Side of Cadwalader Street

Owner	Location	Date	Property Damage	Monetary Loss
Edward Develin	Cadwalader Street, below Master Street	May 6	doors and windows damaged	unknown
Peter Develin	Cadwalader Street, below Master Street	May 6	house damaged	unknown
Hibernia Hose Company	Cadwalader Street, above Master	May 7	building burned down	unknown
Patrick Lafferty	first house north of hose house	May 7–8	house destroyed by fire	unknown

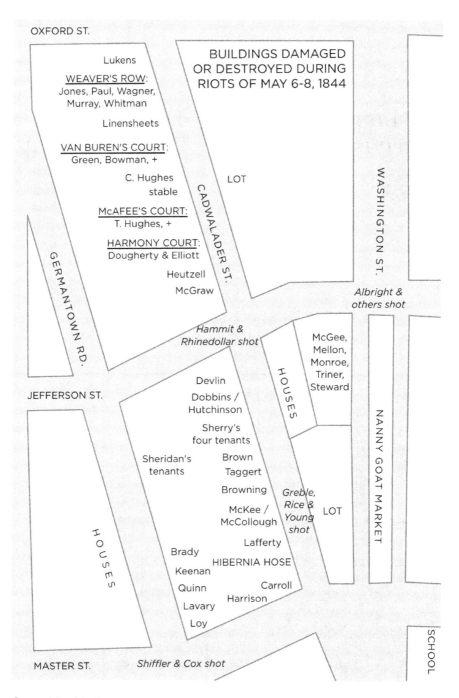

OXFORD ST.

Lukens

WEAVER'S ROW:
Jones, Paul, Wagner,
Murray, Whitman

Linensheets

VAN BUREN'S COURT:
Green, Bowman, +

C. Hughes
stable

McAFEE'S COURT:
T. Hughes, +

HARMONY COURT:
Dougherty & Elliott

Heutzell

McGraw

BUILDINGS DAMAGED
OR DESTROYED DURING
RIOTS OF MAY 6-8, 1844

LOT

CADWALADER ST.

WASHINGTON ST.

GERMANTOWN RD.

JEFFERSON ST.

Albright &
others shot

*Hammit &
Rhinedollar shot*

Devlin

Dobbins /
Hutchinson

Sherry's
four tenants

Sheridan's
tenants

Brown

Taggert

Browning

McKee /
McCollough

HOUSES

McGee,
Mellon,
Monroe,
Triner,
Steward

NANNY GOAT MARKET

*Greble,
Rice &
Young
shot*

LOT

Lafferty

Brady

Keenan

HIBERNIA HOSE

Quinn

Lavary

Loy

Carroll

Harrison

HOUSES

MASTER ST.

Shiffler & Cox shot

SCHOOL

Ownership of buildings that were destroyed during Kensington Riot. Alderman Clark and his brother's houses, St. Michael's buildings and the nunnery are not shown. *Courtesy Torben Jenk.*

Owner	Location	Date	Property Damage	Monetary Loss
John Brown	Cadwalader Street, above hose house	May 7–8	house destroyed by fire	unknown
John Dougherty	Harmony Court, west side of Cadwalader Street	May 8	four houses destroyed by fire	$800.00, plus $200.00 lost by tenants
Charles Elliott	Harmony Court, west side of Cadwalader Street	May 8	three houses destroyed by fire	$1,200.00, plus $150.00 lost by tenants
Bernard Sherry	Cadwalader Street, between Master and Jefferson	May 7–8	four houses (one frame, three brick) destroyed by fire, tenanted by his employees	$3,000.00
John Heinsell	Cadwalader Street	May 7–8	carpenter shop, at rear of property, destroyed by fire	$400.00 to $500.00
John Taggert	Cadwalader Street	May 7–8	house destroyed by fire	unknown
Hugh Develin	Cadwalader Street, second door from Jefferson	May 7–8	house sacked by mob	$300.00

Owner	Location	Date	Property Damage	Monetary Loss
Mrs. Dobbins	Cadwalader Street	May 7–8	ingrain carpet manufactory, with dye house, occupied by Ashton S. Hutchinson	$1,500.00
Patrick McKee	Cadwalader, above Master	May 7–8	frame house, occupied by Owen McCulla	$400.00, McCulla lost $1,000.00

Eight Buildings on East Side of Germantown Road

Owner	Location	Date	Property Damage	Monetary Loss
Mrs. Brady	Germantown, above Master	May 6	two-story frame house ransacked	$100.00
John Lafferty	Germantown, adjoining Mrs. Brady's property	May 6	brick house, slightly damaged	unknown
Michael Keenan	Germantown, above Master	May 7–8	frame house and back buildings destroyed by fire	$500.00

Owner	Location	Date	Property Damage	Monetary Loss
Thomas Sheridan	Germantown, above Master, near Jefferson, possibly a courtyard	May 7–8	one frame house, two brick houses, tenanted by his employees, destroyed by fire	$2,500.00
Patrick Murray	southeast corner of Germantown and Jefferson	May 8	large brick house and store sacked, looted and destroyed by fire	$4,000.00

Six Buildings on North Side of Master Street

Owner	Location	Date	Property Damage	Monetary Loss
John Carroll	northwest corner of Master and Cadwalader, facing Master	May 7	two frame houses, as well as two other adjoining houses, all destroyed by fire, one occupied by widow Harrison	$1,600.00, tenants lost $250.00, Mrs. Harrison lost $700.00 in silver

Owner	Location	Date	Property Damage	Monetary Loss
John Lavary	Master, below Germantown	May 7–8	house stoned on May 6, later destroyed by fire	$2,000.00
James Loy	Master, below Germantown, next to John Lavary	May 7–8	two-story frame house, occupied by Michael Quin, destroyed by fire	$150.00

Nine Buildings on Washington (American) Street

Owner	Location	Date	Property Damage	Monetary Loss
District of Kensington	Washington Street, between Master and Jefferson	May 7–8	Nanny Goat Market, 260-foot-long market house, destroyed by fire	$3,000.00 to $4,00.00
Patrick Magee	corner of Washington and Jefferson Streets	May 8	large brick house, destroyed by fire, possibly second house next door	$1,500.00
John Mellon	west side of Washington Street	May 8	house sacked and destroyed by fire	$1,500.00

Owner	Location	Date	Property Damage	Monetary Loss
James Monroe	west side of Washington Street	May 8	house destroyed by fire	$2,500.00
James Triner	west side of Washington Street	May 8	three-story brick house, destroyed by fire	$1,500.00
William Steward	west side of Washington, below Jefferson Street	May 8	two buildings, one with ingrain carpet manufactory, with looms, wool, etc., destroyed by fire	$4,000.00
Manderson	on Washington Street	May 7–8	building destroyed by fire	unknown

Thirteen Buildings on Second Street

Owner	Location	Date	Property Damage	Monetary Loss
St. Michael's Church	east side of Second Street, south of Jefferson Street	May 8	church and rectory destroyed by fire, cemetery vandalized	$75,000.00

Owner	Location	Date	Property Damage	Monetary Loss
Sisters of Charity, B.V.M.	southeast corner of Second and Phoenix Streets	May 8	nunnery/ seminary destroyed by fire	$6,468.98
Benjamin Hutchinson, Esq.	east side of Second Street, below St. Michael's Church	May 8	one three-story frame and one two-story frame, destroyed by fire	$2,500.00
Francis McCreedy	east side of Second Street, south of Benjamin Hutchinson	May 8	four frames, one large frame known as "Refrectory," one large frame weaving factory, two small frames, all destroyed by fire	$1,800.00
Barney Rice	Second Street	May 7–8	house destroyed by fire, together with adjoining dwellings	unknown
John McAleer	corner of Second and Master Streets	May 7–8	two large brick houses, destroyed by fire, one tenanted by man named Rice	$3,000.00, with Rice lost at $600.00
John/Owen Daley	Second Street, near Master Street	May 7–8	frame house, behind McAleer's house, ransacked and destroyed by fire	$400.00

Owner	Location	Date	Property Damage	Monetary Loss
Joseph Corr	northeast corner of Second and Phoenix Streets	May 8	Temperance Grocery Store, ransacked and looted	$1,500.00

Two Buildings on West Side of Fourth Street

Owner	Location	Date	Property Damage	Monetary Loss
Patrick Clark	southwest corner of Fourth and Master Streets	May 8	house and tavern sacked	unknown
Hugh Clark	first house south of Patrick Clark's house, on Fourth Street	May 8	house sacked, lost of all personal papers, library, notes and accounts, furniture, etc.	$1,000.00

BIBLIOGRAPHY

ARTICLES, BOOKS, PAMPHLETS AND WEBSITES

Address of the Catholic Lay Citizens of the City and County of Philadelphia, to Their fellow-citizens, in reply to the Presentment of the Grand Jury of the Court of Quarter Sessions of May Term 1844, in Regard to the Causes of the Late Riots in Philadelphia. Philadelphia: self-published, 1844.

Battle of the Diamond. http://en.wikipedia.org/wiki/Battle_of_the_Diamond. Accessed December 1, 2012.

Belisle, Orvilla S. *The Arch Bishop, or, Romanism in the United States.* Philadelphia: W.W. Smith, 1855.

Boyle, William J. *The Story of St. Michaels, 1834–1934.* Philadelphia: Press of Jeffries & Manz, 1934.

Camack One-Name Study. http://www.one-name.org/profiles/cammack.html. Accessed December 12, 2012.

Campbell, John H. *History of the Friendly Sons of St. Patrick and of the Hibernian Society for the Relief of Emigrants from Ireland: March 17, 1771–March 17, 1892.* Philadelphia: Hibernian Society, 1892.

Chaos in the Streets: The Philadelphia Riots of 1844. http://exhibits.library.villanova.edu/chaos-in-the-streets-the-philadelphia-riots-of-1844/. Accessed December 12, 2012.

Clark, Dennis. *The Irish in Philadelphia: Ten Generations of Urban Experience.* Philadelphia: Temple University Press, 1973.

Crane, Elaine Forman, editor. *Diary of Elizabeth Drinker.* Boston: Northeastern University Press, 1991.

Davis, Allen F., and Mark H. Haller, editors. *The Peoples of Philadelphia: A History of Ethnic Groups and Lower-Class Life, 1790–1940.* Philadelphia: Temple University Press, 1973.

Eisenhardt, Miriam, et al. "The Five Irish Clusters in 1880 Philadelphia." Unpublished paper, located at the Social History Project, University of Pennsylvania, Philadelphia, PA.

Feldberg, Michael. *The Philadelphia Riots of 1844: A Study of Ethnic Conflict.* Westport, CT: Greenwood Press, 1975.

The Full Particulars of the Late Riots, with a View of the Burning of the Catholic Churches, St. Michaels & St. Augustine. Philadelphia: published at 23 North Second Street (likely self-published), 1844.

Gallman, J. Matthew. *Receiving Erin's Children: Philadelphia, Liverpool, and the Irish Famine Migration, 1845–1855.* Chapel Hill: University of North Carolina Press, 2000.

Gauer, David W. *Vaughan Shipwrights of Kensington, Philadelphia: Their Van Hook & Norris Lineages and Combined Progeny.* Decorah, IA: Anundsen Publishing Co., 1982.

"George Shiffler." 1844 broadside poem, printed and for sale at G.S. Harris, southeast corner of Fourth and Vine Streets, Philadelphia.

Giustiniani, Reverend L. *Intrigues of Jesuitism in the United States of America.* New York: Printed for the author by R. Craighead, 1846.

In The Early Days: Pages from the Annals of the Sisters of Charity of the Blessed Virgin Mary, St. Joseph's Convent, Mount Carmel, Dubuque, Iowa, 1833–1887. Second Edition. St. Louis, MO: B. Herder Book Co., 1925.

Kenrick, Reverend Francis Patrick. *Diary and Visitation Record of the Rt. Rev. Francis Patrick Kenrick: Administrator and Bishop of Philadelphia, 1830–1851. Later Archbishop of Baltimore. Translated and Edited by Permission and Under the Direction of His Grace the Most Reverend Edmond F. Prendergast, Archbishop of Philadelphia.* Philadelphia: self-published, 1916.

"The Kensington Massacre." *The Republic, a Magazine for the Defence of Civil and Religious Liberty*, no. 1 (August 1845).

Kirlin, Joseph L. *Catholicity in Philadelphia.* Philadelphia: John Jos. McVey, 1908.

Lanard, Thomas South. *One Hundred Years with the State Fencibles.* Philadelphia: Nields Company, 1913.

Lannie, Vincent P., and Bernard C. Diethorn. "The Philadelphia Bible Riots of 1840." *History of Education Quarterly* 8, no. 1 (Spring 1968).

Lawlor, Kathryn, editor. *Terence J. Donaghoe, Co-founder of the Sisters of Charity, B.V.M.* Dubuque: IA: Mount Caramel Press, 1995.

Lee, John H. *The Origin and Progress of the American Party in Politics: Embracing a Complete History of the Philadelphia Riots in May and July, 1844…and a Refutation of the Arguments Founded on the Charges of Religious Proscription and Secret Combinations.* Philadelphia: Elliott & Gihon, 1855.

Lippard, George. *The Nazarene; or, The Last of the Washingtonians, A Revelation of Philadelphia, New York and Washington, in the Year 1844.* Philadelphia: T.B. Peterson, 1846.

McAleer, Margaret H. "In Defense of Civil Society: Irish Radicals in Philadelphia during the 1790s." *Early American Studies: An Interdisciplinary Journal* 1, no. 1 (spring 2003): 176–98.

McIntyre, John T. *The Ragged Edge: A Tale of Ward Life & Politics.* New York: McClure, Phillips & Co., 1902.

Mining Community at Avoca, 1780–1880. http://familytreemaker. genealogy.com/users/j/o/h/Mervyn-George-Johnson/FILE/0004text. txt. Accessed December 12, 2012.

Montgomery, David. "The Shuttle and the Cross: Weavers and Artisans in the Kensington Riots of 1844." *Journal of Social History* 5, no. 4 (1972): 411–46.

Moore, Justus E. *The Warning of Thomas Jefferson: A Brief Exposition of the Dangers to be Apprehended to our Civil and Religious Liberties.* Philadelphia: Wm. J. Cunningham, 1844.

The Olive Branch, Or, an Earnest Appeal in Behalf of Religion, the Supremacy of Law, and Social Order: With Documents Relating to the Late Disturbances in Philadelphia. Philadelphia: M. Fithian, 1844.

[Perry, John B.] *A Full and Complete Account of the Late Awful Riots in Philadelphia: Embellished with Ten Engraving[s].* Philadelphia: John B. Perry, no. 198 Market Street. Henry Jordon, Third and Dock Street. New York: Nafis & Cornish, 1844.

Philadelphia City Directories. Philadelphia: A. McElroy, 1837–1845.[Directories were published yearly]

Scharf, John Thomas, and Thompson Westcott. *History of Philadelphia, 1609–1884.* Philadelphia: L.H. Everts, 1884.

The Truth Unveiled, Or, a Calm and Impartial Exposition of the Origin and Immediate Cause of the Terrible Riots in Philadelphia on May 6th, 7th, and 8th, A.D.. 1844. By a Protestant and Native Philadelphia. Philadelphia: Printed by M. Fithian, 1844.

The United States Catholic Magazine and Monthly Review IV, 1845. Baltimore: Printed and Published by John Murphy, 1845.

Verses Composed on the Slaughter of Native Americans, in Kensington, Philadelphia, May, 1844. For Sale Wholesale and Retail at the Cheap Book Store, South Second above Catharine Street; at the Book Stand, S. W. corner of Vine and Second, and at No. 512 North Second Street. Philadelphia, 1844.

Wallace, H.E., and David Webster, editor. *Pennsylvania Law Journal.* Volume IV. Philadelphia: L.R. Bailey, Printer, 1845 (contains Kensington Riot case for John Daley).

Newspapers

Philadelphia Catholic Herald, May 1844.
Philadelphia Inquirer, March 1840, January 1843, January 1844–December 1845.
Philadelphia National Gazette, August 1828, March 1840.
Philadelphia North American, March 1840; January 1843; January 1844–December 1845.
Philadelphia Public Ledger, March 1840, January 1843, January 1844–December 1845.

Note: The author read all articles that had to do with the Kensington Riots for the periods listed above. The dates of the individual articles are too numerous to list. Genealogybank.com offers a searchable database for eighteenth- and nineteenth-century Philadelphia newspapers. These papers were viewed by the author during the summer and fall of 2012.

Government Records

Philadelphia Clerk of Quarter Sessions Court Docket, 1843–1845; Bills of Indictment, 1844–1845; Road Dockets, 1685–1953; Road Petitions, 1685–1919; Road Case Record, 1836–1944. Located at Philadelphia City Archives. These records are helpful for the riot trials, as well as the development of West Kensington area.

Philadelphia Courts. Grand Jury. Minutes, 1844. This jury considered many of the cases arising from the anti-Catholic riots of 1844 in Kensington and Southwark (1 v.). Located at the Historical Society of Pennsylvania within the collection titled "Miscellaneous Government Records. 1664–1950."

Philadelphia Department of Health, Death Records, 1844.

Philadelphia Prothonotary of Common Pleas Court Appearance Docket, 1757–1913; Judgement Docket, 1810–1811, 1819–1874; Execution Docket, 1769–1874. Located at Philadelphia City Archives.

United States Federal Population Census for 1840 and 1850 for District of Kensington, Philadelphia County, Pennsylvania. Accessed on Ancestry.com, summer and fall 2012.

Manuscripts

"Journal of J. Warner Erwin, 1839–1854." http://www.brynmawr.edu/iconog/jwe/jweint.html. Accessed December 1, 2012.

Letter of George W. Ziegler to his wife, dated Philadelphia, September 1, 1844, on his viewing the ruins of St. Augustine's Church. In the collection of Daniel Dailey.

Letter of H. Loomis to his brother L.D. Loomis of Oran, Onondaga County, New York, dated Philadelphia, May 9, 1844, on his thoughts about the military, the mob and Catholics. In the collection of Daniel Dailey.

INDEX

Lippard, George 34
Loughran, Father William 115, 116, 118
Louth, County 19, 20, 22, 23
Lutheran church 52

M

Masters' Estate 18
Masters, Sarah 18, 20
Masters, Thomas 18
Master Street School 36
McCracken, Henry Joy 12
McIntyre, John T. 137
McMichael, Sheriff Morton 82, 108
Methodist 48, 50, 52, 56, 57, 59, 74, 97
Mexican War 104
Monroe Guards 109, 112, 113
Moravian church 52
Moyamensing 37, 43, 44, 60, 76, 135
Munro, Henry 12

N

National Guard 45, 108, 112, 119
nativist field hospitals 107
nativist meeting
  May 3 58
  May 6 62
Nativist Party
  founding in West Kensington 54
  founding of 47
nativists
  arrested 135
  killed 131
  post-riot 126
  wounded May 6 71
  wounded May 7 106
Neumann, (Saint) Bishop John 138
New Catholic Association of Ireland 20
nunnery of the Sisters of Charity 19, 29, 34, 78, 79, 81, 82, 108, 115, 118, 132, 135

O

Orangemen, Order of 12, 13, 14, 23, 102, 103

P

Page, Colonel James 119
Palmer Cemetery 75
parochial school system 138
Paul, John 86, 91, 92, 105, 134, 136
Peep of Day Boys 12, 14
Penn, William 15, 18, 27
Philadelphia and Trenton Railroad 41
Philadelphia Cadets 109, 112
Philadelphia Grays 83, 119
Philadelphia Rangers 104
Phillips, Henry M. 134
Poe, Edgar Allan 41
police force, Kensington established 127
Presbyterian church 12, 52, 137

R

Railroad Riots of 1840–1842, Kensington 41
Ramsay, Nathan D. 80, 81, 82, 108, 118, 131
Rebellion of 1798 12, 14, 38
Reni, Guido 29
Rhinedollar, J. Wesley 65, 91, 96, 101, 103, 105, 131, 137
Rice, Joseph 96, 98, 102, 103, 107, 112, 131, 134, 135
Riot of 1828 38
riot trials 133
Rush, J. Murray 134

S

Second Pennsylvania Volunteers 104
Sherry, James 61, 65, 91, 136, 137
Shiffler, George 73
Shiffler Hose Company 77
Shrieves, John 106
Sisters of Charity, B.V.M. 30, 79, 80, 115

About the Author

Kenneth W. Milano is a historical and genealogical researcher with over twenty years experience in the history of Philadelphia's neighborhoods of Fishtown and Kensington, as well as the metropolitan area of Philadelphia. He was born and raised in Kensington and still lives in that section of Philadelphia, where his mother's German ancestors first arrived from Unterleichtersbach, Bavaria, in 1844.

Milano is a graduate of Northeast Catholic High School (1977) and Temple University (1995), where he graduated *cum laude* from the history department. Milano also has more than twenty years of history in the rare and scholarly bookselling world. He currently works with Michael Brown Rare Americana, LLC, of Philadelphia.

In the mid-1990s, Milano, along with Rich Remer and Torben Jenk, helped to found the Kensington History Project, a community-based historical group that researches, lectures and publishes on the history of Kensington and Fishtown. He is the author of *The Rest Is History*, a weekly local history column that was published in the *Star* newspapers from 2007 to 2011. Milano is the author of numerous books on local history, including *The Hidden History of Kensington and Fishtown* (The History Press, 2010).

In 2003, Milano was inducted into the Philadelphia Archdiocese's Northeast Catholic High School Alumni Hall of Fame. From 2008 to 2010, he served on the board of directors for the Pennsylvania Genealogical Society. Currently, Milano sits on the St. Anne's Historical Committee, where he helps to document the rich Irish history of St. Anne's Church and Cemetery.

Milano still lives in Kensington with his wife, Dorina Lala, and their two sons, Francesco and Salvatore.

CPSIA information can be obtained
at www.ICGtesting.com
Printed in the USA
LVHW080216230620
658769LV00011B/100